STAMPART

15 original rubber stamp projects
for cards, books, boxes, and more

GLOUCESTER MASSACHUSETTS

ROCKPORT PUBLISHERS

Sharilyn Miller

First published in the United States of America
by Quarry Books, an imprint of
Rockport Publishers, Inc.
33 Commercial Street
Gloucester, Massachusetts 01930-5089
Telephone: (978) 282-9590
Fax: (978) 283-2742

Distributed to the book trade and
art trade in the United States by
North Light, an imprint of
F & W Publications
1507 Dana Avenue
Cincinnati, Ohio 45207
Telephone: (800) 289-0963

Other distribution by
Rockport Publishers, Inc.
Gloucester, Massachusetts 01930-5089

ISBN 1-56496-583-x

10 9 8 7 6 5 4 3 2

Designer: Visual Voices, Ejyo Katagiri
Cover photography by Kevin Thomas
All photography by Kevin Thomas, except for
  photos on pages 102, 106, 110, and 114 by
  Tom O'Brien; styling by Eda Lavine; courtesy
  of *Somerset Studio*.

Printed in China.

Dedicated with love and appreciation
to my parents, Allen and Lenore Miller.

CONTENTS

7   Introduction

8   Materials

12   Stamp Basics

16   Altered Surface Treatments

18   Nature Stamping: *Janet Hofacker*

22   Faux Finishes: *Lynne Grant Mohr*

26   Marbled Surfaces: *Lea Everse*

30   Patterned Backgrounds: *Hélène Métivier*

34   Masking, Layering, and Stenciling: *Nathalie Métivier*

40   Gallery of Altered Surface Treatments

46   Artistic Stamping

48   Reverse Stamping: *Lea Everse*

52   Faux Postage: *Moya Scaddan*

56   Deep Thermal Embossing: *Diane Lewis*

60   Stamp Carving: *Sharilyn Miller*

64   Stamping on Acetate: *Linda Yang-Wright*

68   Gallery of Artistic Stamping

74   Mixed Media Effects

76   Metallic Accents: *Lisa Renner*

80   Collage and Decoupage: *Lynne Perrella*

84   Stamped Booklets: *Sherrill Kahn*

88   Miniature Books: *Julie van Oosten*

92   Large-Format Art: *Zana Clark*

96   Gallery of Mixed Media Effects

102   With One Stamp

102   Cranes

106   Grapevines

110   Kookaburras

114   Open Book

118   Glossary

120   Resources

124   Directory of Artists

126   Stamp Credits

127   Acknowledgments

128   About the Author

INTRODUCTION

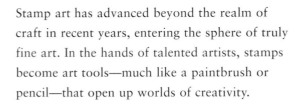

Stamp art has advanced beyond the realm of craft in recent years, entering the sphere of truly fine art. In the hands of talented artists, stamps become art tools—much like a paintbrush or pencil—that open up worlds of creativity.

With the burgeoning popularity of stamping around the globe, a plethora of books on stamping basics has been published. This is the first book to take the reader beyond the basics, into the realm of stamp art.

Why use rubber stamps? The reasons are as varied as the artists themselves. Art stamps free up latent creativity in individuals who have no formal training in drawing and painting. They are useful tools in the hands of experienced professional artists as well. Some of the finest artists working today have turned to rubber stamps to create gorgeous faux finishes, marbled backgrounds, handmade cards, artistamps (faux postage), collages, large-format gallery art, and handmade books.

The contributors to this book will show you how to do the same. Come alongside these talented artists and take your stamping skills beyond craft . . . into the realm of art.

MATERIALS

Before beginning your own pieces of stamped artwork, be sure to familiarize yourself with the range of materials and tools available to today's artists. If you have further questions, consult the Glossary.

Many of the materials you will need can be found at your local crafts and art-supply store, but if they are unavailable in your area, the product manufacturers listed in Resources offer mail-order services worldwide.

Art Stamps

Most art stamps are machine manufactured with a wood mount to grip by hand, a soft cushioning material between the wood and the rubber, and the rubber die itself, which has the raised image that is inked and impressed onto a surface. Some stamps are made with clear acrylic mounts and clear polymer, making it possible to see precisely where your image will be stamped. And some artists opt to carve their own stamps from potatoes, corks, wood, linoleum, and rubber erasers.

Stamp Cleaner

In addition to commercial stamp cleaners, options include pre-moistened towelettes, baby wipes, and paper towels moistened with gentle household cleansers or mild window cleaner. Never wash mounted stamps or submerge them in water, as this will loosen the adhesive holding the rubber to the cushioned stamp mount.

Ink

Archival ink: Ink with a neutral pH level to prevent gradual degradation of the material on which it is used.

Dye ink: Water-based, quick-drying ink that penetrates the paper surface and is therefore not the best choice for scrapbooks and other archival materials. Dye inks may bleed when applied to unsized (absorbent) papers, and they generally cannot be embossed.

Embossing ink: A non-pigmented, slow-drying ink used to emboss, slightly tinted so the artist can see the stamped image long enough to apply embossing powder.

Fabric ink: Ink that has been specially formulated for application to fabric. It sometimes must be heat set with an iron.

Permanent ink: Also known as waterproof ink, permanent ink is used when the artist wishes to apply water-based media after stamping, as it will not smear or smudge. However, it can be difficult to clean from your stamps.

Pigment ink: Pigment ink is fade-resistant, slow drying, and perfect for embossing with clear powder. It lies on the stamped surface and usually must be heat set or embossed to prevent smudging.

Rainbow pad: An economical set of several small pads, each one inked with a different color, arranged in a spectrum to create a single large ink pad. Available in dye or pigment ink.

Re-inkers: Bottles of dye, embossing, or pigment ink that can be used to add ink to dry ink pads. A real money saver for stamp artists.

Paint

Acrylics: Quick-drying, polymer-based media mixed with pigments, best used on fabric or with large, bold stamps.

Cel-vinyl paint: Used by commercial cartoonists, animators, and illustrators, cel-vinyl paints are opaque, vinyl acrylic co-polymer made to be used on clear acetate.

Fabric paint: Many fabric paints can be used with stamps. They are usually water-soluble and permanent when dry. Some must be heat set before the fabric can be washed.

Gouache: A water-based, opaque, pigmented media, available in liquid or cake form.

Oil paint: Although oil paint may be used with care by stampers, a lengthy drying time makes it less than desirable.

Watercolors: A popular choice among stamp artists, watercolors are translucent, pigmented, water-based media available in liquid or cake form. They can be painted directly on a rubber stamp before stamping, or an image can be stamped with permanent ink and then painted over with watercolors.

Markers and Pens

Embossing pens: Pens with embossing ink, available in many colors. Artists write with the pens and then emboss their graceful script with clear or colored powders.

Fabric ink pens: Pens that work on fabric without bleeding, useful for coloring in stamped images.

Markers: All types are available, some water-based, in a multitude of colors and nib widths. They can be used directly on stamps.

Metallic ink pens: Pens with opaque metallic ink are used for a variety of purposes, including creating marbled backgrounds.

Opaque ink pens: Also known as opaque paint markers, these pens are used on clear acetate and other surfaces.

Pencils

Colored pencils: These are used in stamp art after an image has been impressed.

Pastels: Similar to chalk, pastels can be hard or soft, powdery or oil-based. They often are rubbed into papers before stamping to give the surface an antique look.

Watercolor pencils and crayons: After stamping an image with permanent (waterproof) ink, watercolor pencils and crayons can be used to add color. A paintbrush dipped in water is then applied to blend the pigments.

Powders

Embossing powder: Made of tiny plastic pellets too small for the human eye to discern, powders are available in hundreds of colors and in various types such as ultra-fine powders for detail stamping and ultra-thick for deep embossing.

Interference pigment: Metal oxides or powdered mica to add color and sparkle. Interference pigment may be mixed with white glue or acrylic medium to create acrylic paint, or with gum arabic and water to create watercolor. It also can be brushed or sponged on dry and secured with acrylic sealer.

Tools

Brayer: A soft rubber roller used to apply an even layer of ink to detailed art stamps and smooth surfaces such as glossy cardstock. Roll the brayer over the pad in short strokes going in the same direction.

Craft knife: Used to cut out stamped images for paper tole and to trim cardstock and paper. A self-healing cutting mat will protect the work surface as you cut.

Embossing tool: Also known as a heat gun, this is the best hand-held tool for melting embossing powder as it adheres to ink on the stamped surface. Avoid using toaster ovens, hot plates, or light bulbs for embossing; they can be dangerous.

Linoleum cutter: Used to carve stamps from linoleum, rubber erasers, potatoes, and other soft materials.

Ruler: Clear plastic, high-quality rulers are preferable.

Scissors: Now made with decorative edges, including scallops, postal notches, and curves. Always keep sharp.

Sponge: Used to add surface color before stamping or to lightly apply paints and dyes directly to the stamps themselves. Collect an array of sponges with unique textures—sea sponges, makeup sponges, kitchen sponges, and boat sponges are just a few—and wash them thoroughly before and after use.

Stencil: Shaped holes cut out of acetate, paper, or card stock, stencils are used to apply color in various shapes while protecting surrounding areas from its application.

Stamp positioner: Allows artists to position each image precisely. Follow accompanying instructions.

Adhesive

Dry: For most projects, try two-sided adhesive tape, glue sticks, foam tape, or spray adhesive. Or use a machine that applies adhesive to flat items by turning a hand crank.

Wet: Wet adhesives are fine for most papercrafts, but they can buckle the paper if used improperly. Try PVA (white glue) or other acid-free options.

Paper

Machine-made: These papers provide a smooth surface, both porous and non-porous, and are available in a range of colors.

Cardstock: A heavyweight paper used to craft greeting cards and business cards.

Decorative: Includes gift wrap, decoupage paper, marbled paper, and printed paper of all types.

Envelopes: Available in many colors and sizes, but you can make your own with a template (see below). Many stamp artists consider the humble envelope the perfect canvas for their "mail art."

Handmade: Used for collage elements in compositions or for stamping if sizing has been added to prevent the ink from bleeding.

Templates: Templates are used to make custom envelopes, note cards, gift boxes, and other items. Purchase them or make your own templates by taking apart an envelope or box and tracing its form onto decorative paper.

Other Stamping Surfaces

Candles: Stamping on candles is most easily achieved by stamping first on white tissue paper, embossing the images, and then wrapping the tissue around the candle. Apply heat from the embossing tool to the candle surface; the wax will melt slightly, adhering the tissue and causing it to "disappear," leaving behind the stamped images.

Glass: Use acrylics or porcelain paint, and comply with the manufacturer's instructions about oven baking.

Fabric: Muslin is good for experimenting and can yield beautiful results, but silk and denim are other options. Use fabric ink or acrylic paint, and follow the manufacturer's instructions regarding heat setting.

Velvet: To stamp on velvet, mist the fabric surface lightly with water, then lay it nap-down on an upended stamp. Heat the iron on the wool setting without steam, and press it on the velvet over the stamp for about 20 to 30 seconds. When finished, lift away the velvet to reveal the beautiful crushed image. Not all art stamps are made to withstand the heat of an iron; when in doubt, consult the manufacturer.

Wood: Stamping on wood is similar to stamping on paper. Dye inks will soak into porous wood, but pigment inks dry slower and usually can be embossed.

Pottery: Paint pottery first with a primer and then with acrylic or house paint. When the surface is dry, stamp it with acrylic paint or pigment ink, and emboss the stamped images.

Embellishments

Beads, buttons, and charms: Available in thousands of shapes, sizes, and colors, these can be glued onto stamped artwork, threaded and sewn in place, or used as dangling embellishments.

Ribbon and lace: Antique ribbons and laces are favorites; so are sheer, organdy, and narrow ribbons. In addition, wide ribbon made of natural materials can be stamped and heat set.

Found items: Organic and inorganic materials—what some may call litter—abound in every neighborhood. Includes scraps of paper, ticket stubs, bits of wire, feathers, a

STAMP BASICS

Art stamping is a form of relief printing and, as such, is a skill easily mastered with practice. The best stamp artists understand that a stamp is a tool—much like a paintbrush or a pencil—and the only way to improve dexterity is by stamping, stamping, stamping! Work on a firm, even surface such as a table top. Choose your papers and cardstock beforehand, have several stamps available, and make sure that all of your ink pads, colored pencils, scissors, embossing powders, and other tools and materials are within reach. Once you begin a stamping session, you won't want to be interrupted.

Ink and Stamp

Begin by selecting a stamp and inking the rubber image evenly with dye-based or pigment ink. Markers also may be used. Ink the stamp evenly to make an attractive impression.

When using a raised ink pad, place the pad on the table and tap the art stamp onto it. If the stamp is very large, turn it over and tap the ink pad onto the rubber image. Another option is to use a brayer to cover the stamp surface from edge to edge with an even layer of ink.

Use colored markers to ink specific areas of the rubber image with the hues of your choice. Because ink from markers dries faster on rubber stamps than do dye- or pigment-based inks from pads, re-moisten the ink by holding the rubber stamp near your mouth and exhaling a burst of warm breath—this will revitalize the colors before stamping. By continuing to moisten the stamp with your breath, you may get several stampings from one application of ink.

Next, press the stamp firmly onto the paper. Be sure not to rock the stamp as you press down, because the edges will smudge. How hard should you press? Well, not too hard. But not too soft, either. As with most art techniques, practice is the best teacher. Lift the stamp straight up from the surface with one quick motion. Pigment ink is sometimes sticky; you may have to hold the paper down with your other hand while lifting the stamp.

Colored pencils and markers

Once your stamped image has dried on the paper, use colored pencils and markers to flesh it out. Stamp with waterproof ink if you plan on coloring in the image with markers, or emboss the image first. When an image is embossed, the raised areas form little plastic bumps on the paper, making it safe to color within and around the lines with water-based media.

Embossing

Thermal embossing raises an image above the printing surface. This technique requires an embossing agent, usually a powder, which is heated with an embossing gun that blows very hot air out of a pointed nozzle. Embossing powder consists of tiny plastic pellets which the embossing gun melts.

To emboss, first stamp an image onto the surface using clear embossing fluid or pigment ink. Dye-based inks, including most colored markers, will not emboss. Sprinkle embossing powder on the stamped image, covering it completely while the ink is still damp. Shake off the excess embossing powder and save it for later. Heat up an embossing gun for several seconds and hold it a few inches above the powdered image until you see the powder melt. An important safety tip: Emboss in a well-ventilated area, and try not to inhale the fumes from the powder as it melts. The fumes are visible and have a distinct odor.

When finished, the stamped image will have a raised surface. Many embossing powders are available; depending on which one you use, the embossed image may be shiny, matte, iridescent, or glittery. Ultra-fine powders are available for embossing finely detailed stamp images, and ultra-thick powders are used in deep thermal embossing.

Masking

Masking allows you to stamp several images over each other without marring the previously stamped images. This technique is simple and versatile, but the resulting artwork can be amazingly detailed.

First, select cardstock for a finished project, and stamp the image you want to appear in the foreground. Next, create a mask by stamping the same image on plain paper and cutting it out just inside the outermost lines.

Place the mask over the foreground image originally stamped. Select another stamp for a background image, ink its rubber surface, and stamp the surface as desired, occasionally overlapping part of the masked foreground image. Use a positioner, if desired. You needn't worry about ruining the foreground image, because it's covered with the mask.

Rubber Brayer

Most relief-print artists are familiar with brayers, which are made of rubber and are similar to small paint rollers. Depending on the techniques used, you can achieve varying results, including borders, edges, repetitive patterns, and washes of color.

Simply roll the brayer in the same direction over an ink pad, using a roll-and-lift motion. Avoid using a back-and-forth motion, which will ink only the same spot on the brayer. Roll the brayer onto the project as desired. Ink specific areas, lines, or patterns on the brayer with color markers, too.

In addition to using a brayer to apply color directly onto a project, use it to ink finely detailed stamps to ensure even coverage and, therefore, a more perfect print.

Layering

Stamp artists add dimension to their work by stamping an image, cutting it out, and then layering it on top of the project using foam tape or silicone caulking to raise the image from the background.

Paper tole, a form of three-dimensional decoupage, also is achieved in this way. Stamp and color the same image several times on similar paper. Then cut out the stamped and colored images. Note which parts of the image seem to be in the foreground, and cut these parts out of some of the cutouts. Next, layer the cutouts onto a cardstock base using silicone caulking as an adhesive. The bottom layer is the entire image; each subsequent layer will be smaller and smaller, until you are left with the tiniest detail cutouts in the foreground. For added realism, curl the paper cutouts over a pen or a pencil before adhering them.

Stamp Positioning

Using a stamp positioner is an easy-to-learn skill that helps make the difference between sloppy work and elegant, precise stamping. The best positioners on the market include a stamp positioning tool and a sheet of clear acrylic to stamp on. Tracing paper may be substituted for the acrylic sheet.

First, place the acrylic sheet in the corner of the stamp positioner, then align the edges of the wood-mounted (inked) stamp with the corner of the tool. Stamp the image firmly and lift off. You now have a template for positioning.

Next, position the template wherever you want to place your stamped image—perhaps right next to another stamped image or in the center of a piece of stationery. Once you are satisfied with the placement, align the corner of the stamp positioner with the acrylic sheet, then remove the template.

Ink your stamp and align it within the corner of the positioner as before, and stamp firmly. Lift off. Now you have a perfect impression, precisely where you want it.

Stamp Maintenance

With care, your stamps will last for years, particularly if you remember that sunshine is an art stamp's worst enemy. Light and heat from the sun will quickly dry out and crack the rubber, rendering it incapable of absorbing ink. Store your rubber stamps, image-side down, in a cool, dark place.

To prolong a stamp's life, clean it after each impression. The easiest way is to moisten a paper towel with a very weak mixture of water and stamp cleaner or household window cleaner, and then pat the stamp onto the paper towel to remove the ink. Pat again on a clean, dry paper towel.

Some artists prefer to clean their stamps with commercially available baby wipes (non-alcohol). The cleansing agent not only is gentle, but the moisturizers help keep the rubber supple.

ALTERED SURFACE TREATMENTS

Before most stamp artists set rubber to paper, they consider the printing surface. A marvelous selection of commercially made paper is available today. Nonetheless, many artists prefer to make their own background papers to complement their work.

Janet Hofacker prepares her nature journals with a random sponging of inks, thin acrylic washes, and metallic paints, while Lynne Grant Mohr takes meticulous care applying layers of pigment ink to glossy cardstock. Marbled backgrounds are Lea Everse's specialty. She likes nothing more than a surprise to reward her efforts, often allowing the media its own way— with stunning results.

Hélène Métivier makes patterned papers by applying pigment ink pads directly to cardstock. In her easy, elegant way of transforming ordinary paper into something special, she then stamps images in a random fashion. Nathalie Métivier uses a similar but more complicated technique, employing a series of masks and stencils to create intricate layers of color.

Nature Stamping

Janet Hofacker's nature journal allows her to experiment with background surface treatment and new color combinations, while also providing a safe place to experiment with mixed media. On each journal page, she blends stamped images with collaged elements such as cutouts from catalogs or bits of tree bark, leaves, and flowers gathered on nature walks. In addition to using manufactured stamps, she also makes imprints of leaves and feathers. Yes, it's possible to stamp using materials found in nature. Leaves, bark, lichen, rocks, seashells—virtually anything with texture can be inked, printed, and preserved on paper.

ARTIST: **Janet Hofacker**

Getting Started

Nature journals require artists to exchange the quiet confines of the studio for a walk outdoors. When possible, seek out new vistas—perhaps a mountainside trail frequented by bird watchers or a stream bed in a park you've never visited before. As you walk, make note of the surrounding colors, textures, and scents. Pick up leaves, feathers, and other natural elements with which to stamp. However, take some precautions: Avoid poisonous vegetation and plants on your local conservation list.

Materials

Stamps

Blank, unlined journal

Feathers, bark, and/or dried vegetation

Ink pads in assorted colors

Acrylic glazes (or acrylic paints)
in assorted colors and metallics

Colored pencils and pastels

Sea sponge

Dry adhesive

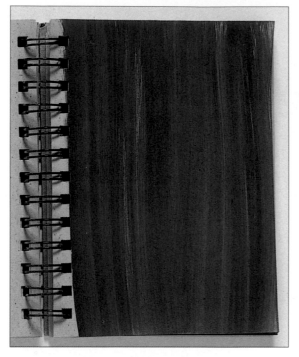

1 Prepare a blank, unlined journal by sponging or painting each page using thinned-down acrylic glazes or paints. Glazes are preferable since they do not need to be thinned down too much and are less likely to buckle the paper. To add interest, layer the background colors, allowing each application to dry before further additions.

2 To print with natural elements such as feathers or leaves, clean them, if necessary, with a lightly dampened sponge and allow them to dry completely. Apply a little color to one side of the specimen by pressing it onto an ink pad or sponging it lightly with acrylic paint. Press the specimen gently but firmly onto the journal page, taking care not to move it. Carefully lift the specimen and let the stamped image dry. Lightly accent the page with metallic gold wash.

Journal Tips

- For a unified look, use the same color scheme and background paint on the facing pages of each spread of your journal.

- The same leaf often can be reused if handled gently. Immediately remove the paint or ink with a damp sponge, and pat the leaf between paper towels to dry.

- Lightly coat the finished pages with protective acrylic spray, allowing each spread to dry thoroughly before spraying the next.

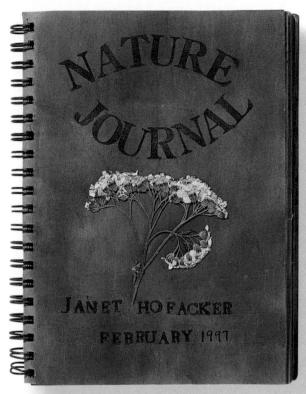

3 Continue adding interest to the page. Apply
another metallic wash, such as copper. Adhere
collage elements—a feather, as shown here, or bits
of torn paper, pressed flowers or leaves, or thin layers
of tree bark.

Variation

Hand write or use alphabet stamps to print brief inspira-
tional quotes, poetic phrases, or field notes describing
the origin of a specimen. Introduce fauna into your
composition with manufactured stamps of bird and
insect images. Create soft backgrounds with pastels or
colored pencils.

Faux Finishes

Lynne Grant Mohr's delicate manipulation of pigment inks on glossy cardstock easily achieves the luxurious appearance of marble and stone. The resulting sensuous, textured background is perfect for stamping. Mohr's approach is careful and deliberate; her method will appeal most to those artists who prefer a controlled application of color and design. Use pigment inks for this project—dye inks will not work with the technique. Generally, dye inks permeate the surface of most papers and cardstock, while pigment inks lay on the surface and must be heat set or sealed with an acrylic spray.

ARTIST: Lynne Grant Mohr

Materials

Stamps: leaf, texture

White glossy cardstock

Pigment ink pads in beige, deep pink,

ocher, brown, terra cotta, light green

Soft rubber brayer

Sea sponge

Acrylic protective spray

Getting Started

Assemble the materials and prepare your work area by laying down some newsprint, as pigment inks are messy and may stain some surfaces. You will need several pieces of glossy cardstock to practice with. Remember that if you make a mistake at any time during the process, you can start over by re-wetting and rubbing off the pigment ink.

1 Starting with the lightest color, roll the brayer over the beige ink pad several times to thoroughly coat it with pigment ink. Bray the cardstock with short strokes in a random pattern. Then roll the brayer over the deep-pink ink pad, and bray the cardstock again in the same manner. Continue as above with the ocher ink, massaging and blending the colors together with firm, short strokes.

2 To create darker values, use a soft sea sponge to dab on more deep-pink and ocher ink. Sponge on brown ink in a few select areas. Then roll the brayer over the cardstock again, this time with a little less pressure, being careful not to smooth out too much sponged-on texture. To add interest to the composition, use an accent color such as terra cotta. Dab it on lightly, and feather it a bit with the sea sponge.

3 To add veins, use the edge of torn cardstock. Lightly scrape the edge back and forth through the layers of ink until you reveal a light streak. Feather the edges with a sponge. Allow the ink to set for about 30 minutes before proceeding. For added interest, stamp the entire surface with a texture stamp and brown ink.

Ink Tips

- Try adding a little color to the leaf veins by moistening the scrap paper with dark ink such as dusky brown.

- Coated glossy cardstock will not absorb pigment ink, so you can continue to manipulate the surface until it is sealed with acrylic spray. Be careful not to smudge foreground images before sealing the artwork. If a design is less than successful, feel free to remove all of the color and return to the original glossy paper surface; simply re-moisten the color with additional pigment ink and firmly rub it off.

4 To add foreground images, create a mortise mask the same size as the image area by tearing a piece of paper to form a hole or frame. Lay the mask on the finished cardstock, and buff off some of the ink within the framed area. For an antique look, rub very lightly to remove just the top layers of ink. Try sponging on a bit of light-green ink through the mask.

5 Now stamp the foreground decorative images using a dark, contrasting color. If you have a stamp positioner, use it to stamp over the light-green ink design. To protect and seal the artwork, spray it with several light coats of acrylic protective spray. Allow it to dry, and adhere the artwork to a folded card or frame it for display.

Variation

Using the same faux background and leaf colors, vary the design with a different leaf stamp—in this case, bamboo leaves. Stamp over the light-green leaf image with gold ink instead of red to add depth and shimmer to the leaves. For a middle-ground image to add interest to the faux background, stamp terra-cotta Chinese calligraphy characters in loose columns.

Marbled Surfaces

Luscious, marbled background papers are easy to make with just a few materials. While the process may appear to be difficult and time-consuming, Lea Everse's marbled background technique is actually quite simple. Beautiful, saturated colors of wet ink flow gracefully together on black glossy cardstock when the artist tilts the surface. Voila! Marbled backgrounds, which can be used to create attractive greeting cards such as the one shown here.

ARTIST: **Lea Everse**

Materials

Stamps: background, bird

Glossy cardstock

Card base

Metallic pigment ink markers in gold, pink, blue, purple

Black pigment ink

Black embossing powder

Gold thread

Two-sided tape (or other dry adhesive)

Foam tape

Spray mister

Distilled water

Sea sponge (or crumpled plastic wrap)

Embossing tool

Scissors (straight or decorative edge)

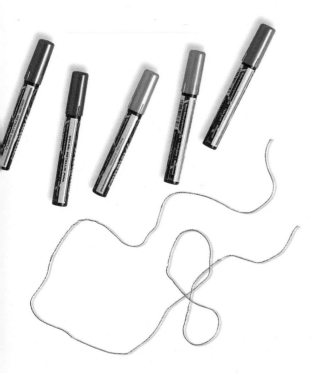

Getting Started

Only a few materials are needed for this project, but metallic pigment ink markers are absolutely essential. Black glossy cardstock will render the most dramatic effects, but white cardstock is another option. Stamp artists are very particular about the cardstock they use, but if a specific color or finish is unavailable, it's easy enough to spray ordinary cards with glossy paint.

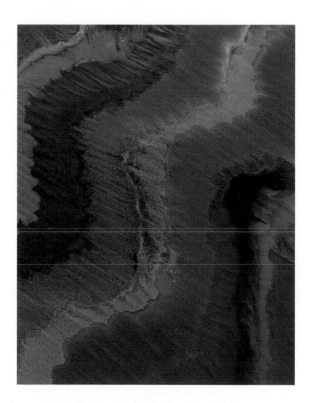

1 Trim the cardstock to 4.25" x 5.5" (10.5 cm x 14 cm). Using a spray mister, lightly spritz the surface with distilled water until lightly dampened. Color the middle of the card with gold metallic pigment ink. Quickly, before the water evaporates, cover the surface completely with additional colors of metallic pigment ink.

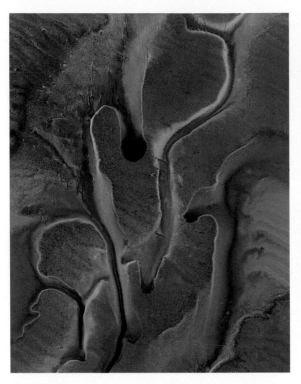

2 Tilt the card, which causes the wet metallic inks to flow and gives the piece its distinctive marbled look. Once the entire surface is colored, spritz again with water and touch lightly with a sea sponge.

3 When the card is completely dry, stamp and emboss the marbled surface using a background stamp, black ink, and black embossing powder. Heat with an embossing tool.

Marbling Tips

- When covering the dampened card surface with metallic pigment ink, try braying the ink together or creating patterns by dragging a feather, small paintbrush, or cat's whisker through the wet ink.

- Use an embossing tool or hair dryer to hasten drying of the marbled background before stamping.

- If an attempt at marbled paper is less than satisfactory, cut the cardstock into strips to be used later for paper weaving or assembling a unique modern-art design.

4 Use two-sided tape to mount the marbled background card onto coordinating layers of black and gold cardstock, graduated in size and cut with straight or decorative-edge scissors. For the card's central imagery, prepare decorative cutouts such as the birds shown here, which were stamped and embossed on prepared marbled paper.

5 Mount the central images to the background paper with foam tape and embellish with gold thread. Adhere the design to a card base with two-sided tape.

Variation

To reveal more of the marbled background, use a single figurative stamp, such as this woman with a fish, instead of an overall pattern.

Patterned Backgrounds

Making beautiful papers for stamping backgrounds is much easier than it looks. With pigment inks, stamp artists can transform ordinary cardstock or paper into beautifully patterned, undulating surfaces.

Canadian artist Hélène Métivier begins with ordinary beige cardstock and, with a few strokes of pigment ink pads, creates papers perfect for stamping. In this project, a range of stamps decorate richly colored squares of paper which are arranged to make an intriguing cover for a scrapbook.

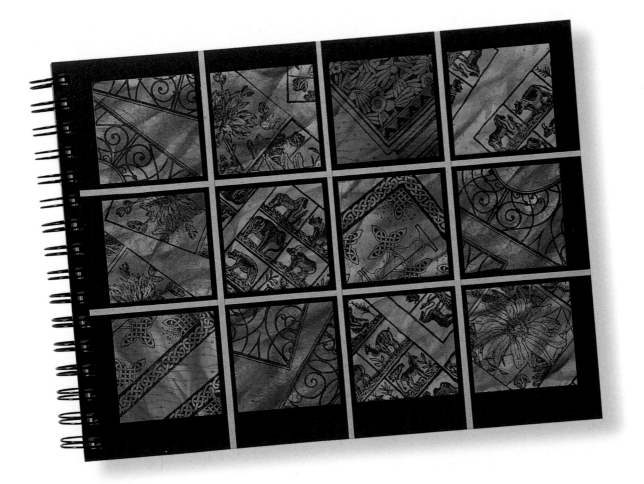

ARTIST: **Hélène Métivier**

Getting Started

For this project, use pigment inks—which lie on the paper's surface and dry very slowly—to achieve the subtle look of brushed-on pastels. Dye ink pads also may work, but they make the desired effect more difficult to attain. When choosing inks for each surface, consider analogous color combinations such as yellow, green, and yellow-green, or red, violet, and orange.

Materials

Assorted stamps

Light-color cardstock (or paper)

Pigment ink pads in black, gold, assorted colors

Scrapbook
(approximately 10.75" x 8.25"
[27.5 cm x 21 cm])

Two-sided tape (or other dry adhesive)

Scissors (or craft knife and cutting mat)

Ruler

Acrylic protective spray

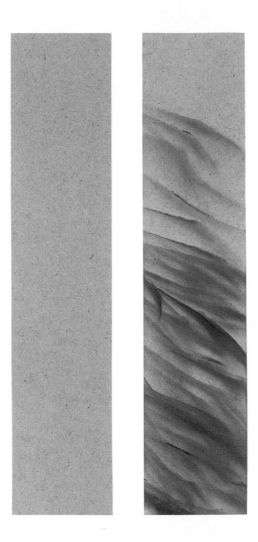

1 Measure and cut the cardstock into three 2" (5 cm) strips at least 8" (20 cm) long. Gently brush each strip with pigment ink pads, choosing analogous colors and applying each pad directly to the surface using soft, S-shaped strokes. Spread on the lightest hues first.

2 Continue layering pigment ink in a swirling pattern, ending with the darkest colors. Allow the ink to dry.

Pigment Application Tips

- For each background, restrict the number of pigment inks to two or three to avoid muddied colors.

- As an alternative approach, apply pigment ink to a sponge, and sponge the paper with soft, gentle strokes.

3 Use various stamps to cover the strips with random patterns. Stamp with ink that contrasts well with the background—black and gold pigment ink are good choices. Finish the surface with acrylic protective spray.

4 Cut the strips into 2" (5 cm) squares, and arrange them in a pretty pattern on the scrapbook's front cover, leaving .25" (.5 cm) between the squares. Adhere them with two-sided tape. Add interest by applying a grid of narrow strips of contrasting paper between the squares.

Patterned Backgrounds 33

Masking, Layering, and Stenciling

This project calls for the basic skills necessary to every stamp artist desiring to increase the complexity of his or her work. Stamping, of course, comes first. But masking and stenciling skills are no less important. Finally, layering images is key to creating a multidimensional pattern. The following piece's appealing design incorporates all of these techniques. Canadian artist Nathalie Métivier limits her color palette to emphasize the butterfly stamp, which she also designed.

ARTIST: **Nathalie Métivier**

Getting Started

This is a complex project requiring several intricate steps, so gather all the needed materials and have plenty of repositionable glue and correction tape on hand before you begin. Read the instructions through at least once before commencing the project to avoid confusion. Foreground images will be stamped in warm colors, contrasting with cool-color backgrounds that appear to recede.

Materials

Stamps: butterfly, leaf, flower

Tan cardstock

Paper

Pigment ink pads in greens, oranges, assorted light colors

Permanent black ink

Two-sided tape (or other dry adhesive)

Repositionable glue stick

Correction tape

Scissors (or craft knife and cutting mat)

Acrylic protective spray

1 Trim tan cardstock to 8.5" (22 cm) square and use permanent black ink to stamp a butterfly three times along the center vertical axis. On a piece of thin paper, prepare paper masks by stamping the same butterfly three times and cutting out the images. Apply a thin layer of repositionable glue to the back of the masks, and place them as shown over the stamped butterflies. Begin coloring in the background by gently rubbing pigment ink pads directly on the cardstock.

2 Using correction tape, mask off the edges of the cardstock. Cut a rectangular piece of paper to mask the center, and adhere as shown. Use permanent black ink to stamp four leaves onto the cardstock, and then make eight paper leaf masks. Adhere masks onto the stamped leaves, and artistically position and adhere the other four masks to create silhouettes.

3 Apply pigment ink to both sides of the design, rubbing it in liberally and using various shades of green or similar colors. The masks will protect the foreground images and borders from ink.

4 Remove the rectangular mask from the center, cut it in half lengthwise, and adhere the pieces to the design as shown. Apply pigment ink pads to the center of the design, including orange and green. The butterfly masks will protect the stamped images beneath them.

5 Remove the two narrow rectangular masks and the masks of the silhouette leaves. Rub on a bit of orange or red ink for contrast. Remove the outermost row of correction tape and stamp a series of small leaves to create a narrow border.

6 Remove all remaining masks and tape, and stamp a little flower in each corner of the masked-off frame. Now create stencils by stamping three butterflies on paper and carefully cutting them out. Discard the stamped centers and separate the stencils.

Masking and Stenciling Tips

- Accurate paper masks and stencils are critical, so be sure your scissors or craft knife blades are extra sharp.

- Begin your own designs by deciding which stamps will ultimately predominate. Stamp and mask these images first, and cause them to advance by filling them in with colors that are in contrast with and darker than the background.

- Masking and stenciling techniques also work well for airbrushing. Instead of applying pigment ink to cardstock, lightly airbrush paint over the masks and through the stencils.

7 Apply glue to the stencils and lay each one over a stamped butterfly on the cardstock. Gently apply contrasting pigment inks to the stamped butterflies through the stencils. Remove the stencils and finish by randomly stamping a few small images in very light ink (pink, light blue, gold) onto the overall design. Coat lightly with acrylic protective spray, and mount the finished artwork on graduated layers of cardstock.

Variation

By using lighter colors to advance the foreground image, a single flower, surrounded by darker leaves, appears to pop out of this masked and layered composition.

GALLERY OF
Altered Surface Treatments

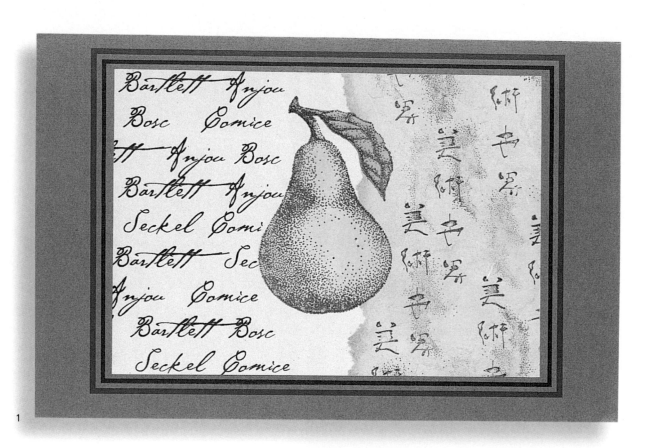

1

LYNNE GRANT MOHR

1 *Pear*
Chinese calligraphy, rubber stamped

2 *Collage*
text, postage stamp, metallic ink

3 *Feather*
cardstock, script, stamp images

4 *Snapshots*
sponge, computer-generated border

2

3

4

1 **JANET HOFACKER**
painted, stamped wooden box with found items

2 **NATHALIE MÉTIVIER**
stamping, masking, layering, and stenciling on cardstock

3 **MARYSE CARRIER**
collage of strips of stamped cardstock

4 **JANET HOFACKER**
wood, metallic paint

2

42   *Altered Surface Treatments*

3

Dream
no small dreams.

4

1 **LEA EVERSE**
cardstock, beads

2 **MARYSE CARRIER**
collage of strips of stamped cardstock

3 **LYNNE GRANT MOHR**
rubber stamps, pigment ink,
glossy cardstock

4 **LEA EVERSE**
stamped, embossed image on
marbled cardstock

1

2

3

4

ARTISTIC STAMPING

Stamping artistically means using rubber stamps in unusual ways, combining stamp images with handmade papers, or creating artist books, faux postage, and mail art. The traditional use of stamps to make simple greeting cards is fine, but many more options are available to artists who use stamps in their artwork.

Lea Everse's reverse-stamping technique cleverly mimics the look of monoprinting with far less time and effort. If miniature artwork is your passion, consider making faux postage (also known as arti-stamps) with help from Moya Scaddan. Diane Lewis's technique of deep thermal embossing is popular with stamp artists everywhere; no wonder, when it's so easy and the results are so gorgeous.

Custom-designed, hand-carved art stamps also fall into the realm of artistic stamping. I learned to make rubber stamps from master carver Julie Bloch of Hurleyville, New York. Using ordinary erasers and linoleum cutters, you, too, can make your own custom stamps.

Finally, Linda Yang-Wright stamps on acetate and applies opaque markers and cel-vinyl paint (traditionally used by cartoon artists) to transform the images into striking three-dimensional works of art.

Reverse Stamping

Reverse stamping is very similar to monoprinting, an age-old technique requiring the artist to ink a smooth glass surface, remove portions of the ink from the glass, and transfer the inked design to paper. Monoprinting is beautiful, but the procedure is messy and can be difficult to master.

ARTIST: **Lea Everse**

Getting Started

Begin this project by assembling the necessary materials in a protected work area with easy access to soap and water for quick cleanup. Be prepared to wash the brayer before the ink dries on the roller after inking the cardstock surface. In addition, stamps must be cleaned thoroughly after each impression in the wet ink. Since reverse stamping uses liquid pigment ink, beware of staining clothing or other items.

Materials

Stamps: lotus and Egyptian woman

Glossy cardstock

Matte cardstock

Card base

Liquid pigment inks in blue and black

Clear embossing powder

Decorative thread

Two-sided tape
(or other dry adhesive)

Foam tape

Brayer

Embossing tool

Scissors (or craft knife
and cutting mat)

Ruler

1 Squeeze blue liquid pigment ink directly onto a piece of black glossy cardstock. A little ink goes a long way, so start with a very small amount, adding more as needed. Use a large brayer to smooth out a thin, even layer of ink to cover the card surface.

2 Press the clean (un-inked) lotus stamp firmly onto the inked surface. Twist the stamp slightly (about 1/16" [1.5 mm]) to cut through the ink down to the card-stock. Lift the stamp and clean it. Continue stamping the inked surface, cleaning the stamp after each impression. Sprinkle the surface with clear embossing powder, tap off the excess, and heat set with an embossing tool.

3 When the blue lotus-stamped card is dry, trim it to a 4.5" (11 cm) square. Cut three additional layers of cardstock for the finished greeting card: a 3.5" (9 cm) rust-colored square, and a 3.75" (9.5 cm) square and 4.75" (12 cm) square of black glossy cardstock.

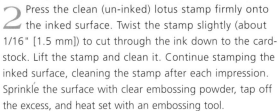

Reverse-Stamping Tips

- When choosing commercially made stamps for this technique, select images with few details or fine lines. Reverse stamping works particularly well with hand-carved stamps, since they typically have straightforward designs.

- As an alternative to non-absorbent, glossy cardstock, try reverse stamping on handmade paper, stationery, watercolor paper, or professional-grade printmaking paper. Also experiment with numerous color combinations. For instance, try spreading red pigment ink on gold cardstock.

4 On a separate sheet of rust-colored cardstock, stamp the Egyptian figure three times and the lotus design four times with black pigment ink. Emboss and cut out the images.

5 Assemble the layers of square cardstock according to size, beginning with the largest piece and ending with the rust-colored square on top. Adhere the layers together with two-sided tape and embellish the top square with a border of decorative thread. Use foam tape to mount the cut-out images. Adhere the design to a card base with two-sided tape.

Variation

Make another background layer for the card using the same technique with slight variation. Here, a wavy background design is reverse stamped on cardstock on which two colors of pigment ink—blue and rust—are blended together.

Faux Postage

Anyone who has ever admired the diminutive art of postage stamps will understand the prevailing popularity of faux postage, that is, stamped designs on perforated paper mimicking the size and shape of government-issued postage stamps. Also known as artistamps, faux postage obviously cannot be used in lieu of paid postage. Artistamps are a recognized art form, most often applied to envelopes as a decorative element or purchased in numbered sheets by avid collectors. Moya Scaddan of Sorrento, Western Australia, uses beautiful stamps made especially for creating faux postage. Another option is to use any stamped design that fits within the parameters of a typical postage stamp.

ARTIST: **Moya Scaddan**

Materials

Stamp: Cave of the Bulls faux postage

Cardstock

Paper

Ink pads (dye or pigment ink) in black, brown

Pencil, pastels, and watercolor markers

Two-sided tape (or other dry adhesive)

Perforating (tracing) wheel

Sea sponge

Scissors (or craft knife and cutting mat)

Ruler

Getting Started

Creating a sheet of artistamps requires lightly sketching a regularly spaced grid, so select an accurate ruler and a sharp pencil or fine-line pen. Some artists prefer using a computer with a drawing program to lay out uniform sheets of stamps or to design faux postage from scratch.

Simulating the look of commercially produced stamps, artistamp projects involve perforating the paper. Inexpensive perforating or tracing wheels with serrated edges are available in most fabric stores.

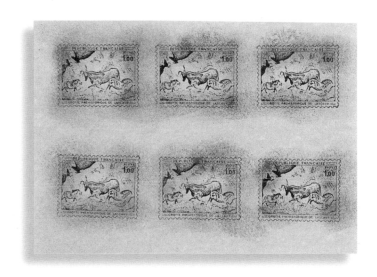

1 Stamp the faux-post image six times onto buff-colored paper. Sponge around the edges of the stamped images with a sea sponge and some dye ink, or rub pastels in natural earth tones onto the paper.

2 Cut out the stamped images, trimming away the stamped-on perforation border. Set aside.

3 Cut a second sheet of buff-colored paper to approximately 6" x 8.5" (15 cm x 22 cm), unevenly tear the edges, and sponge on brown ink for an aged appearance. In the center, lightly pencil in a grid with six 1.75" x 2 1/8" (4.5 cm x 5.3 cm) rectangles. Use a watercolor marker to color the center of the rubber faux postage stamp, and lightly stamp outside of the six rectangles.

Production Tips

- Perforating can be done not only with a rolling perforation wheel, but also with a professional stamp perforating machine. Another option is to perforate the paper using a sewing machine with a thick, unthreaded needle.

- Artistamps are meant to be shared with others, so keep the original sheet and have copies made to send to mail-art friends.

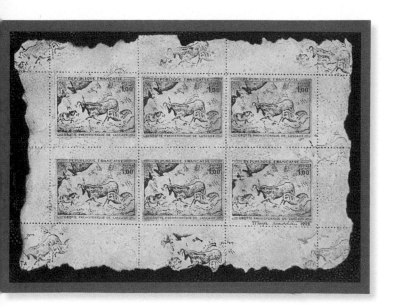

4 Using a perforating wheel, roll along the penciled-in grid lines all the way to the paper's edges. Use two-sided tape to adhere a cut-out stamp within each of the six rectangles in the grid. Mount the finished sheet of artistamps on cardstock backing.

Variation

Play with a variety of stamps and colors. Here, an ample border is randomly stamped with images related to the faux stamps' theme. As an alternative to making a sheet of identical artistamps, create a sheet in which the artistamps are each unique but share a similar theme and color scheme.

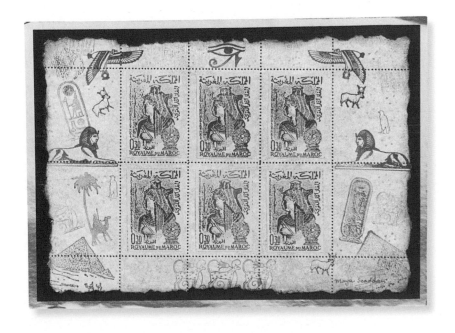

Deep Thermal Embossing

Few stamping techniques have more dramatic results than deep thermal embossing, also known as multi-layered embossing. The procedure is similar to encaustic stamping, but embossing ink and powders are substituted for wax. Diane Lewis has mastered the method of melting multiple layers of embossing powders to create a thick, glossy surface for stamping. A three-dimensional impression is made by pressing an inked stamp deep into the smooth, heated surface—thus the name of the technique. Artists and jewelry designers enhance and embellish the melted powder by dropping in colored embossing powders, iridescent pigments, small beads, or miniature seashells.

ARTIST: **Diane Lewis**

Getting Started

This technique requires special thick embossing powders designed specifically for deep thermal embossing. All consist of large, plastic crystals that melt into puddles when heated. Protect your art room by placing a large box lid upside-down on a flat surface. While embossing, place the cardboard square inside the lid, since crystals inevitably scatter when you begin heating the first layer of powder.

Materials

Assorted stamps

Cardboard

Cardstock

Decorative papers

Pigment or embossing ink pads
in black, terra cotta, paprika, copper

Interference pigments

Embossing powders (regular and thick)

Embossing tool

Two-sided tape (or other dry adhesive)

Wet adhesive

Embellishments: thread, beads, wax seal

1 Prepare a deeply etched, bold-lined stamp by saturating the rubber image with black pigment ink (dye ink will not work). Set aside. Cut out a 2.5" (6 cm) square of cardboard. Rub pigment ink pads directly onto the cardboard, using two or three similar colors such as terra cotta, paprika, and copper.

2 While the ink is still wet, dip the cardboard into thick embossing powder. Gently shake off the excess, and heat the surface with an embossing tool until the powder is completely melted. While the previous layer is still very hot, apply additional layers in the same manner until the surface is thick, glossy, and smooth. Three to four layers should be sufficient; however, some artists apply as many as 18. While heating the top layers, sprinkle a small amount of interference pigments in the wet powder.

Embossing Tips

• Thick embossing powder is now available in clear, bronze, gold, interference blue, black, and platinum. Apply a few layers of clear powder before adding colored embossing powders.

• To give the finished stamped image drama, use black, gold, or silver pigment ink on the stamp's surface.

• Sometimes the melted powder will crack after cooling and hardening, which makes an interesting effect that can be enhanced by rubbing dark pigment inks into the cracks. If you prefer a more perfect surface, reheat the cracks with an embossing tool to make them disappear.

3 While the surface is still wet, carefully press a stamp deep into the melted powder. Hold the stamp firmly until the powder has cooled somewhat. Remove the stamp, which should not be difficult since it previously was coated with pigment ink. To finish the artwork, run a piece of 1/8"-wide (.3 cm) two-sided tape around the edge of the cardboard and cover the tape with tiny gold beads.

4 Prepare collage materials for the base of the composition. Cut out four layers of cardstock in analogous colors to complement the central image. Tear and cut pieces of decorative paper, and stamp or rub them with chalks or interference pigments. Emboss some of the pieces' torn edges using wet adhesive and embossing powders. Assemble the composition, layering the cardstock base and adhering pieces of decorative paper and the embossed cardboard. Embellish your artwork with beaded threads sealed with stamped wax.

Stamp Carving

Carving your own art stamps is a fun way to add images to your collection. Fashioning stamps from rubber erasers is similar to wood-block cutting, but it's much faster. The basic skills can be learned in just a few minutes. Once you have carved a few simple designs, you may want to expand your skills by carving large-scale images from soft printmaking blocks. For inspiration, turn to the Gallery of Artistic Stamping to see the remarkable, large-scale work created by award-winning artist Anne Bagby.

ARTIST: **Sharilyn Miller**

Materials

Rubber eraser, 1.5" x 3" (4 cm x 8 cm)

Source imagery

Paper

Nail-polish remover

Cotton balls

Linoleum-cutting tool

Stamping ink

Access to a photocopier

Getting Started

Purchase rubber erasers with the consistency of firm cheese, such as the high-quality, white erasers found in art-supply stores. For source material, trace the leaf shown here for your first project. In the future, select carving imagery from the copyright-free, black-and-white illustrations in clip-art books, typically available in bookstores and libraries. Or draw your own images by hand, starting with basic geometric shapes such as circles, squares, and stars.

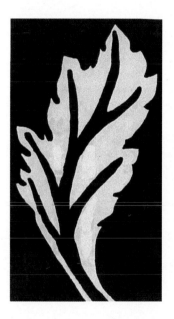

1 Use a carbon-based photocopier to enlarge or reduce the image to a size that fits within the rubber eraser's parameters. Cut out the photocopied image, and place it face-down onto the back of the eraser.

2 Use nail-polish remover, which interacts with the carbon on the photocopy, to transfer the image to the eraser. Soak a cotton ball with remover, and rub the wet ball for a few seconds over the back of the photocopy. Rub in only one direction to avoid distorting the image. Lift a corner of the photocopy to see if the image has transferred to the eraser. If not, replace the corner and continue rubbing the photocopy with the polish-soaked cotton ball. Once the image has transferred, remove and discard the photocopy.

3 Carve out the white areas of the eraser with a linoleum-cutting tool with interchangeable blades. Starting with the finest blade, carefully trim around the image and carve out tiny detail lines and dots. Use wider blades to carve away larger portions of the eraser, taking care not to weaken the stamp by undercutting the image. When carving curved lines, it's easier to turn the eraser than the linoleum-cutter blade.

Carving Tips

- Most erasers are 3/8" to .5" (approximately 1 cm) thick, so they can be carved on the front and back. Some artists also carve tiny border images on the sides of erasers.

- Those with drawing skills may use a ball-point pen or permanent-ink laundry pen to draw an image directly onto the eraser, without going to the trouble of transferring a photocopied image. When drawing letters on the eraser, be sure to write them backwards.

- Once eraser carving has been mastered, try carving larger images from battleship linoleum or soft printmaking blocks available at art-supply stores. Many soft, durable materials can be carved and made into stamps: bottle corks, pencil erasers, soft wood.

4 Test the carved image by inking it well and stamping it on scrap paper. Some artists prefer a rough-cut look, reveling in the stray lines and jagged areas of the image. Others prefer clean lines for perfect repeat stamping. Continue carving away unwanted areas until the image is satisfactory.

5 Create a finished piece using the stamp's simple, graphic image in an artful design. This greeting card is fashioned from handmade paper with flower petals embedded in the pulp. The hand-carved leaf image is stamped in gold and embossed along the card's right edge, as well as stamped onto a separate piece of paper in magenta and turquoise, embossed with clear powder, cut out, and adhered to the cover.

Variation

Experiment making a range of hand-carved stamps, from fruit to decorative imagery. When creating letters or words, write them out normally, enlarge or reduce to an appropriate size, and lay the photocopy face-down on the eraser as described above. The letters will transfer backwards to the eraser, which will print a correct image once the letters are carved.

Stamping on Acetate

Ingenuity and craftsmanship are the keys to using finely detailed art stamps to their best advantage. For this unique project, Linda Yang-Wright uses acetate—an inexpensive art material—to transform her stamping into a fine art worthy of framing. Her method mimics that used by Hollywood artists who meticulously painted each cel of a cartoon in the days before computer-aided animation.

ARTIST: **Linda Yang-Wright**

Materials

Floral stamp

Clear vinyl acetate

Cardstock

Permanent black ink pad

Cel-vinyl acrylic paints and brushes,
or opaque paint markers

Two-sided tape

Getting Started

Art-supply stores are the best sources of clear acetate, but it also can be obtained from photography studios or graphic designers as well as architectural firms, which often discard acetate scraps. Cel-vinyl paints are not as easy to come by, but opaque markers can be found through mail-order craft suppliers. Or substitute gouache paint, an opaque watercolor.

1 Using permanent black ink, stamp a floral image onto acetate. When the ink is dry, flip over the acetate and begin coloring the back of the stamped image with cel-vinyl paint or opaque markers. Start with the finest details, such as the flower stamens and leaf veins. Take your time, since these details will show clearly in the finished piece. Allow each color to dry before proceeding with the next.

2 Continue adding layers of color, focusing on highlights and shadows. The colors may overlap as long as the colors applied first have dried.

3 Color in the largest areas last. The first layers of paint or marker will mask any colors applied over them, so don't worry about overlapping. Occasionally turn over the acetate to check on your progress. Eventually all areas of the flowers and leaves should be colored.

Acetate Stamping Tips

- Rubber stamps with very fine lines work well on acetate. Take care to hold the stamp firmly when pressing down, since acetate can be slippery.

- Images stamped on clear acetate can be easily reversed, giving artists more design options. To reverse a stamped image, do not turn over the acetate before beginning the coloring process. When the image is completely colored and dry, flip over the acetate and the stamped image will appear to be reversed.

4 Once you are satisfied and the coloring is dry, flip over the acetate and lay the design face up on a piece of gold metallic cardstock cut slightly larger than the design's border. Mount with two-sided tape.

5 Continue assembling the piece by adhering the stamped, mounted image to layered squares of black, green, and gold cardstock. Adhere the piece onto a frame of clear acetate which is bordered by a larger frame of green cardstock edged with gold.

Variation

Background and border papers, colors, and textures have enormous influence on any finished piece's appearance, but particularly so when the stamped material is acetate. Experiment with black, white, patterned, and collaged papers. Pastels and metallics render a soft, elegant look, while brighter colors make a bolder statement.

GALLERY OF
Artistic Stamping

2

1

LINDA YANG-WRIGHT

1 *Bean Dream*
   acetate, powder, fabric paint,
   permanent ink

2 *Morning Glory*
   acetate, permanent ink,
   colored papers, fabric paint

3 *Hibiscus Frame*
   acetate, opaque markers, cardstock

3

1

2

1 ANNE BAGBY
Spring Bulbs
acrylics and watercolors on canvas,
with hand-carved stamps used for
repeat imagery

2 ANNE BAGBY
Outward Bound
acrylics and watercolors on canvas,
hand-carved stamps

3 DIANE LEWIS
sponged, stamped cardstock with
deep thermal embossed centerpiece

3

1 **JULIE VAN OOSTEN**
  faux postage and cancellation stamps, used
  postage stamp, cardstock, mulberry paper

2 **TRACY MOORE**
  series of faux postage stamps

3 **MARTHA THURLOW**
  stamped velvet bags with string handles

3

MIXED MEDIA EFFECTS

Mixed media implies variety—and there is plenty to be had in this section. Stamp artists can make everything from handmade books to framed artwork using an eclectic assortment of materials.

Start with the eye-catching metallic effects of Lisa Renner's greeting cards, which incorporate unusual media such as wire and thin sheets of copper with cardstock stamped and treated with metallic embossing powders. If you love collage, Lynne Perrella's stamped notebook will spur your imagination. This designer takes art stamps to a new level by combining their beautiful imagery with decoupage, metallic paints, and found objects.

Two artists featured in this section combine stamping skills with their interest in making books by hand. Sherrill Kahn's easily constructed stamped booklets feature covers in which fabric paints, crimped paper, and beads are exquisite complements to art stamps of petroglyph figures. Julie van Oosten's miniature handmade books have hard covers and spines, and her technique of collage stamping renders a subtle background print perfect for bookbinding.

Finally, Zana Clark's passion for taking stamping beyond cards is evident in her large-format art. By combining stamp imagery with a torn-paper collage, you, too, can make framed artwork of your very own.

Metallic Accents

Marking a special occasion by stamping and coloring a personalized greeting is much more fun than buying a ready-made card, and the results will be treasured by the recipient. When the card incorporates shimmery metallic effects, the sense of value is heightened even further. Shiny copper and gold metallics against black cardstock are a striking combination in this project from stamp artist Lisa Renner. She combines unusual papers with her stamping and embossing techniques to make exquisite mixed-media collage cards worthy of framing.

ARTIST: **Lisa Renner**

Getting Started

For this project, purchase a thin sheet of copper and a piece of copper cardstock from your local craft store. If copper-colored cardstock is not available, spray-paint ordinary paper or cardstock with inexpensive automobile touch-up paint found at hardware stores.

Materials

Stamps: human figure, spiral, marble, papyrus

Cardstock

Lightweight cardboard

Card base

Thin copper sheet

Pigment inks in black, gold, bronze

Thick embossing powders in black, metallic copper, metallic gold

Embossing tool

Embossing stylus

24-gauge copper wire

Beads and other embellishments

Two-sided tape

1 Cut out a 5" x 7.5" (13 cm x 19 cm) piece of copper cardstock and two pieces of black cardstock, one 6" x 8" (15 cm x 20 cm) and the other 2.5" x 5.5" (6 cm x 14 cm). Stamp the marble texture stamp on the copper cardstock and the papyrus stamp on the smaller black cardstock, and emboss using metallic copper embossing powder. On the large piece of black cardstock, stamp the spiral and marble texture stamps and emboss with metallic gold embossing powder.

2 Stamp the woman's figure in black ink in the center of the thin sheet of copper. Emboss with black powder, and heat set with an embossing tool until the ink puffs up. Once the copper sheet has cooled, indent it with a metal stylus, forming an outline around the stamped figure and small points on the surrounding copper surface.

Embellishing Tips

- In addition to incorporating metal beads and wire into your composition, consider including orphan earrings, broken bits of jewelry, watch parts, and computer circuit boards.

- Experiment with the number of metallic embellishments and their arrangement. Sometimes, less is more.

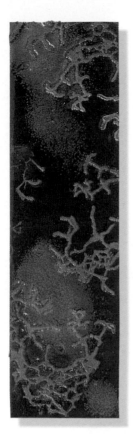

3 Prepare the narrow rectangle for the card's left side by cutting a 2" x 7" (5 cm x 18 cm) piece of lightweight cardboard. Follow the procedure described in the Deep Thermal Embossing chapter, applying thick embossing powders that are heated and re-heated until a hard layer of melted powder covers the surface. While the thick powder is still hot, press a pre-inked marble stamp into it to create a deep impression.

4 Allow the deep-embossed rectangle to cool. Meanwhile, string 24-gauge copper wire with a few beads. Wrap the copper wire around the rectangle, incorporating a metal star or other embellishments into the design. Assemble the composition and mount on a card base using two-sided tape.

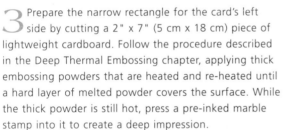

Variation

Try stamping the figure in a thin layer of clay instead of metal. Attach to a strip of copper and thin heavy cardstock layered with colored and embossed paper. To balance the composition, wrap rolls of colored paper with delicate copper wire.

Collage and Decoupage

As you gain confidence with rubber, ink, and paper, add collage elements to your artwork and use the collaged paper to make one-of-a-kind decoupaged items such as the journal featured in this chapter. Lynne Perrella first makes a collage of overlapping art-stamp images, adding torn strips of handmade paper to enhance the design. After reproducing her collage using a color photocopier, she adheres the copies to the cover of a composition book to make a delightful journal.

ARTIST: **Lynne Perrella**

Materials

Assorted stamps

Student's composition book, 7.5" x 9.75"
(19 cm x 24.5 cm)

Plain and handmade paper

Marbled or other decorative paper

Corrugated paper

Ink pads in black and assorted colors

Metallic acrylics

Metallic spray paint

Pastels

24" (61 cm) of 5/8" (1.5 cm) ribbon, for ties

12" (30 cm) of .25" (.5 cm) ribbon, for bookmark

Charm embellishments

Leather or suede scraps

Dry adhesive (two-sided tape or a glue stick)

Contact cement

Sponge

Craft knife and cutting mat

Getting Started

Since the collage you make in this project will be photocopied, the quality of paper you use is not important. Try stamping on plain, white bond paper or flattened, brown paper bags. At the copy shop, consider having the collage reproduced on acid-free paper. The cost will be a bit higher, but acid-free paper is the preferred archival material for long-lasting artwork.

1 Use art stamps, pastels, metallic acrylics, spray paints, and colorful inks to create a visual collage on paper slightly larger than the cover of a student's composition book. For added interest, layer irregular shapes of torn handmade paper between the stamped images. Take the finished design to your local copy shop and have two color photocopies made for the journal's front and back covers.

81

2 Use dry adhesive to adhere the color copies to the composition book's outside front and back covers. Use a sharp craft knife to precisely trim the edges. Cut a piece of corrugated paper to about .75" x 9.75" (2 cm x 24.5 cm), spritz it with metallic spray paint, and glue it to the front cover about .25" (.5 cm) from the spine. Cut the 5/8"-wide (1.5 cm) ribbon into two 12" (30 cm) strips for ties. Center a ribbon on the outside edge of both the front and back covers, and glue down an inch of each one.

3 Create a bookmark by gluing an inch of the .25"-wide (.5 cm) ribbon to the top of the inside back cover, placing the ribbon parallel to and roughly an inch from the spine. Cut two pieces of marbled paper to fit the inside front and back covers and adhere with dry adhesive.

Collage Tips

• If a collage composition seems bland, use pastel crayons to add colorful flourishes of free-hand squiggles.

• When reproducing the collage for your journal, make extra copies to have on hand for future projects such as decorative envelopes, wrapping paper, gift bags—whatever your imagination conjures up.

4 Tear a piece of handmade paper into an attractive shape, stamp randomly, and adhere it with dry adhesive to the center of the front cover. Affix a centerpiece to complement the overall design: a charm, piece of discarded jewelry, antique key, or, as shown here, a collage sandwiched between soldered pieces of glass.

5 To create four corner covers and two anchors for the ribbon ties, use a very sharp craft knife to cut thin scraps of leather or suede into the desired shape and size. Try stamping your leather scraps first with permanent ink. Affix the corners and anchors to the front and back covers with contact cement. Finish your journal by sponging metallic acrylics along the front cover's edges.

Variation

This collage adhered to a large envelope offers a glimpse into the art form's many opportunities for creativity. Add texture by combining stamped images with natural elements such as feathers and dried leaves, or personalize your collage by incorporating copies of family photographs, letters, and other mementos.

Stamped Booklets

At first glance, Sherrill Kahn's stamped booklets may seem complicated and time-consuming to make. But nothing could be further from the truth. Taken in steps, this project can be completed in less than an hour, making it perfect for children and beginning book artists. Once you've mastered the basic "petroglyph" booklet shown here, develop your own cover design using other creative shapes and embellishments.

ARTIST: **Sherrill Kahn**

Materials

Stamps: petroglyph figures, spiral

Heavy cardstock

Bond paper

Large sponge

Bottled acrylic paints in turquoise and blue

Metallic copper paint

Bone folder

Bottles with fine applicator tips

Brush for painting details

Dry adhesive

Glue stick

Paper towels

Water container

Craft knife and cutting mat

Access to a long-arm stapler

Getting Started

Car-wash and boat sponges work well for this project, since they are inexpensive, can be found in most hardware and grocery stores, and are good for painting because they never dry out. To prepare the sponge for stamping, cut it into 1.5" (4 cm) pieces, some in precise squares, others in ragged shapes.

One special booklet-making tool is needed: a long-armed stapler. Many print shops will allow customers who purchase products or services to use their staplers.

1 To create the booklet cover, cut two pieces of burgundy cardstock measuring 5" x 10" (13 cm x 25 cm). Fold one of the sheets in half, and use turquoise acrylic paint to stamp a petroglyph figure on the right front edge. Let the image dry.

85

2 Open the folded cardstock and use a craft knife to cut around the right-hand side of the stamped figure, leaving a 1/8" (.3 cm) border. Paint a metallic copper border along this right side of the stamped image. Fold and adhere the second sheet of cardstock to the inside with a glue stick. Once dry, unfold the cover and cut the edge as before, this time leaving a 1/8" (.3 cm) border around the metallic copper border. Using blue acrylics, stamp another petroglyph figure to the left of the main figure and a series of spiral stamps on the inside back cover. When the stamped acrylics are dry, sponge-paint the front and back cover. Stamp additional petroglyph figures on the front and back of the booklet.

3 Prepare the booklet's pages by cutting six pages of bond paper to approximately 5" x 8" (13 cm x 20 cm). Fold each page in half, separately, using a bone folder for a crisp fold. Insert the papers inside each other and then inside the booklet cover, aligning the folded edges with the inside "spine" of the book. Carefully unfold the booklet and place it face-down on a table. Using a long-arm stapler, staple two or three times along the fold.

Booklet-Making Tips

• To disguise the staples on the outside cover, paint over them lightly. To hide the inside of the staples, glue small, stamped pieces of paper over them. Allow the book to dry flat before folding again.

• If a long-armed stapler is unavailable, bind the booklet by poking four holes in the spine with a large embroidery needle. Then string embroidery floss, weaving thread, or book-binding thread through the holes and tie knots to hold the pages together.

4 Add finishing touches to the cover. Outline the middle figure with copper metallic paint in an applicator bottle with a fine-nozzle tip. Use short strokes of the paint for more control. With a fine brush, paint a turquoise checkerboard pattern around the right edge of the first stamped figure.

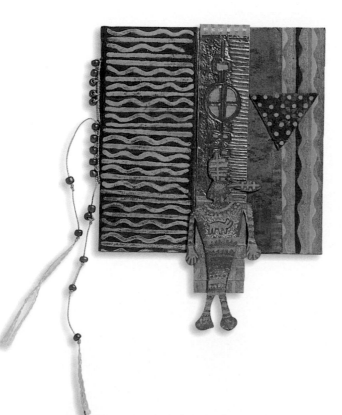

Variation

Make booklets using a variety of stamps and paint treatments. Add touches of whimsy by cutting out stamped figures and mounting them so they hang off the cover's edge. Use decorative thread and beads to embellish the booklet's spine.

Miniature Books

After mastering the technique for making a stamped, stapled booklet, the next logical step is creating a more complex small book with hard covers and a spine. The result is similar to a full-scale, bound book, except with the charm and allure of a miniature object. In this project, Julie van Oosten combines her passion for miniatures with her love of stamping. Because of the book's miniature size, its pages are glued rather than hand-stitched. The cover is embellished with art-stamped papers and ephemera for an old-time, nostalgic appearance.

ARTIST: Julie van Oosten

Materials

Assorted stamps

White bond paper

Cream-colored paper

Decorative paper

Heavy cardstock

Low-moisture archival adhesive,
such as bookbinder's glue

Small bottle with fine-tipped nozzle

Bone folder

Craft knife and cutting mat

Fine ribbon

Sponge

Archival waterproof ink pads in
 black, red, green

Embellishments

Gold wax

Getting Started

Prepare by pouring the glue into the small bottle with a fine-tipped nozzle. This will make it much easier to apply tiny amounts of glue.

When choosing papers and embellishments, look for items with complementary colors. For instance, if you intend to stamp your papers in green and red ink, choose a bookmark ribbon and cover decorations with similar colors.

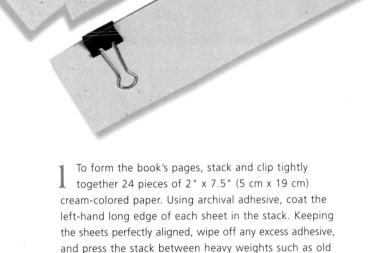

1 To form the book's pages, stack and clip tightly together 24 pieces of 2" x 7.5" (5 cm x 19 cm) cream-colored paper. Using archival adhesive, coat the left-hand long edge of each sheet in the stack. Keeping the sheets perfectly aligned, wipe off any excess adhesive, and press the stack between heavy weights such as old books or bricks wrapped in craft paper. Leave for at least two hours or until dry.

2 Make endpapers by cutting two 4" x 7.5" (10 cm x 19 cm) pieces of decorative paper and folding them in half lengthwise with the decorated side in. Glue down the back of one endpaper's right-hand folded side to the top of the stack of pages, and the back of the other endpaper's left-hand folded side to the bottom of the stack. Press firmly and allow to dry. Using a craft knife and mat, cut the stack of pages into three 2.5" (6 cm) sections. Set aside two of the small stacks of pages to use in future book projects.

3 Create collage-style paper for the book cover by stamping several images on white bond paper using black ink. Use a photocopier to reduce the paper to 75 percent, sponge on red and green waterproof inks, and set aside to dry.

Book-Making Tips

- When embellishing the cover, use decorative items such as charms and sealing wax or found objects such as feathers.

- Experiment with making books of various dimensions. The width of the spine is determined by the thickness of the book's inside pages and endpapers. The pages should be ever so slightly smaller than the covers; if necessary, when the pages are inserted in the book, trim them using a rotary cutter and cutting mat.

4 Cut two 1.75" x 2.5" (4.5 cm x 6 cm) pieces of heavy cardstock for the covers and one thin .25" x 2.5" (.5 cm x 6 cm) strip for the spine. Trim the cover paper to 3.75" x 5.75" (9.5 cm x 14.5 cm), and lay it face down. Position the spine and covers in the center of the cover paper, leaving a .25" (.5 cm) gap on either side of the spine, and adhere. Add support by gluing a 2" (5 cm) square piece of scrap paper onto the cardstock covers and center spine. Then press the paper flat, working a bone folder into all the crevices. Let dry.

5 Miter the corners of the cover paper by cutting them at an angle. With the inside of the cover facing you, fold the cover paper over the edges of the cardstock and adhere. Use a bone folder to smooth out any bubbles, and press the book cover open flat for half an hour while it dries.

6 Position and glue fine ribbon along the spine for a bookmark. Place the pages inside the cover of the book. Glue the outside endpapers to the inside book covers, and quickly remove any excess glue with a slightly damp sponge. Press the book under weights overnight. Embellish the front cover by adhering decorative items, and rub the pages' edges with gold wax to simulate gilding.

Large-Format Art

Stamp artist and designer Zana Clark's mission is to persuade stampers everywhere to go beyond greeting cards. To this end, Zana teaches her students to use stamps, handmade papers, and picture-frame mats to assemble large-format artwork that can be framed and proudly displayed. Substantive mixed media compositions such as the one featured here rely on one or two large, bold stamps that are used in repeat patterns and for the central image.

ARTIST: **Zana Clark**

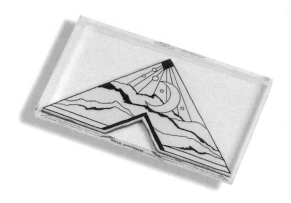

Getting Started

In addition to selecting an engaging stamp design worthy of repetition in your composition, make sure the papers used for the background collage complement the stamped images. Also choose an art mat that will set off the finished design to best advantage; neutral colors, such as white, black, taupe, gray, or beige, often work best.

Materials

Large art deco stamp

Black mat-board frame with gold inner mat, 16" x 20" (41 cm x 51 cm) with an 11" x 14" (28 cm x 36 cm) opening

Frame and protective glass, 16" x 20" (41 cm x 51 cm)

Mat board or other firm substrate, at least 12" x 15" (30 cm x 38 cm)

Cardstock

Handmade papers

Ink pads in assorted colors

Metallic gold embossing powder

Embossing tool

Chalks, pastels, colored pencils

Dry adhesive

Paper towels

Sharp scissors or craft knife and cutting mat

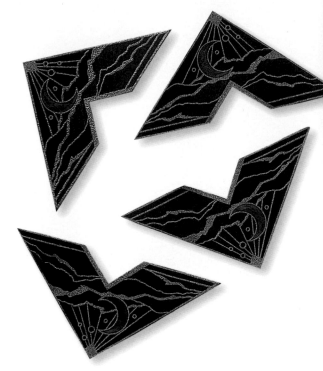

1 Stamp the mat several times with a large art deco image. Emboss the stamped areas with metallic gold embossing powder, and heat set with an embossing tool. Use chalks, pastels, and colored pencils to color in the stamped images.

2 Stamp the same image seven times on black cardstock. Emboss, color, and cut out the images. Set aside.

Composition Tips

• When designing your own composition, incorporate an odd rather than even number of stamped cutout images.

• Don't be afraid to overlap the foreground cutout images over the mat, since this can add a dynamic twist to your artwork.

3 Tear handmade papers into interesting shapes, and arrange them in an 11" x 14" (28 cm x 36 cm) collage on the mat board or other firm substrate. When the composition is aesthetically pleasing and works well with the decorated mat frame, adhere the papers to the substrate. Arrange the stamped cutout images in the foreground.

4 Mat the compostion as shown, and choose a frame that enhances your artwork. To protect the finished piece from sun damage, consider placing it behind glass with ultraviolet screening.

Variation

Achieve a completely different look with a pretty floral stamp, pastel color scheme, and mat board with a round opening.

GALLERY OF
Mixed Media Effects

1

2

1 SHERRILL KAHN
metallic ink, card stock, fabric

2 SHERRILL KAHN
metallic ink, card stock, fabric,
braided thread, beads

3 JULIE VAN OOSTEN
miniature stamps, dye inks,
cardstock

4 JULIE VAN OOSTEN
journal with old-style stamps
on cardstock with
polymer clay centerpiece

3

4

1

1 LYNNE PERRELLA
overlapping stamp images, photo-transfer, pastels, found objects

2 SHERRILL KAHN
metallic ink, cardstock, metal

3 LISA RENNER
cardboard, paper, clay, ribbon

2

3

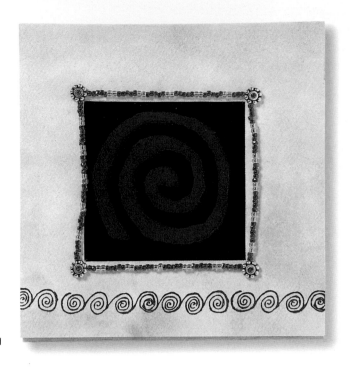

1

1 MARTHA THURLOW
stamped velvet, beads

2 SHERRILL KAHN
metallic ink, cardstock

3 LISA RENNER
clay, wire, beads, papyrus

2

3

With One Stamp
CRANES

Large stamps with repeat patterns, such as this cranes stamp, are known as background stamps. They are used most often to print beautiful background images on cardstock or paper before stamping a larger central image. The cranes stamp pictured here was given to seven artists who were told to create "anything—the sky is the limit!"

Cranes stamped art from bottom left: *Seashell Frame* by Jill Post Fasken; *Framed Mirror* by Sandra Moertel; *Cherry Blossom Kimono* and *Silver Kimono* by Lea Everse; *Japanese Cranes* by MaryJo McGraw; *Collage Crane* and *Bookmark* by Jill Post Fasken; *Porcelain Box* by Michele DeMayo; *Crane Tiles* by Lynne Grant Mohr; and *Ribboned Book* by Sylvia Valle.

Framed Mirror
Sandy Moertel

Emboss the cranes stamp in silver on gold lightweight paper. Mold the paper to a framed mirror, and adhere it with glue.

Porcelain Box
Michele DeMayo

With green dye ink, stamp the lid of a round porcelain box with the background cranes stamp. Stamp the sides of the box with a grass stamp. Spray the porcelain box and lid with two light coats of acrylic sealer. Allow to dry overnight before rubbing chalk lightly on the sides of the lid; then spray again to seal.

Silver Kimono
Lea Everse

Using gold and silver powders, emboss the cranes background stamp on black paper. Run an embossing pen around the edges of the paper and emboss them with gold and silver. Adhere this piece to layers of cardstock in this order: black, gold, black. Mount this to specialty decorative paper, then to more black, gold, and black papers. On specialty decorative paper, emboss the kimono stamp with silver and gold powders, and cut it out. Adhere the kimono to the card with foam tape, and embellish it with a black tassel and a wax seal.

Seashell Frame
Jill Post Fasken

Emboss the cranes stamp in black on the shiny side of silver craft foil. Color in with transparent acrylics (customarily used on glass and found in the hobby section of craft stores), and allow to dry. Cut the foil to the size of a picture frame. Apply spray adhesive to the back of the foil, and mold it to the frame, wrapping it around and smoothing with your fingers. Spray with acrylic sealer. Stamp seashells on water-color paper, heat set them with an embossing tool, watercolor the image, and cut it out. Shape curls in the paper with your fingers and mount it to the center of the frame with foam tape. Embellish the bottom-right corner of the frame with raffia, copper thread, and stones.

Beribboned Booklet
Sylvia Valle

Stamp and emboss the cranes background stamp in gold on black linen cardstock. Trim and fold it into a booklet. Insert a small pad of paper or sticky-notes inside. Emboss the central image in gold on black linen cardstock, trim it around the edges, and adhere it to shiny gold cardstock, then to the booklet. Adhere ribbon to the booklet, wrap, and tie.

With One Stamp
GRAPEVINES

The fruits of creativity come to the fore when the same set of rubber stamps is pressed into the hands of several different artists. Grapes, vines, and flowers are popular images with decorative artists, and the bold, flat designs lend themselves well to stamping in clay, on paper bags, and wood.

Grapevines stamp art, from left: *Goodie Bag* by Robin Dudley-Howes; *Notecard Holder* by Sherry Barncastle; *Golden Harvest* by Anna Leisa Ely; *Sheer Bow* and *Framed Artwork* by Jill Post Fasken; *Antique Wooden Book* by Lisa Renner; *Vintage Card* by Shelley Rymer; *Candy Cone Party Favor* by Robin Dudley-Howes; *Glorious* by Lea Everse; *Treasure Chest* by Lisa Renner; and *Napkin Ring With Napkin* by Robin Dudley-Howes.

Framed Artwork
Jill Post Fasken

Make molds using polymer clay with each stamp. Press Paperclay into baked molds. Gently pull out of mold and press into frame in desired pattern. Allow to dry completely. Fill in any cracks with spackle, and let dry. Paint with acrylic paints, glazes, and metallics. Seal with acrylic spray.

Goodie Bag
Robin Dudley-Howes

Stamp vines and grapes on a brown paper bag using green and purple ink. Antique with a tonal applicator stamp or a sponge. To make the fan, fold the top about halfway down in accordion style. Pinch the sides of the top fold together and staple. Fold over. Embellish with a jute bow.

Sheer Bow
Jill Post Fasken

Stamp vine and grapes on white, wire-edged, sheer ribbon. Tie into a bow with coordinating colored ribbon.

Antique Wooden Book
Lisa Renner

The wood book is antiqued with products from Modern Options. To prepare wood, brush primer onto the surface. Brush on two coats of Blonde Bronze Metallic Surfacer. Sponge on Instant Iron, leaving some of the metallic surface showing. Brush on Instant Rust, and set aside. Brush Copper Topper Metallic Surfacer on black cardstock. Lightly sponge on Patina Green. Stamp grapevine. Heat set. Deckle the edges and brush adhesive around them. Deep emboss with bronze powder. Adhere to a thin sheet of copper with two-sided tape. Mount assembly to a slightly larger piece of black cardstock. Press image of grapes into polymer clay and bake. Apply Rub n Buff Gold Leaf to surface. Glue to top of book cover. Drill three holes at spine edge. Attach together with gold rings. Embellish rings with polymer clay triangles wrapped with copper wire. Note: For this project, allow each application or coat to dry before applying the next.

Treasure Chest
Lisa Renner

This project uses faux finish products from Modern Options. Prime a small wooden trunk with primer/sealer. Brush on Copper Topper Metallic Surfacer. Let dry. Sponge on Patina Green, and let dry. Lightly sponge on Burgundy Tint, wiping off any excess. Dab on gold acrylic paint to highlight selected areas. Spray surface with gold glitter paint. Emboss grapevine leaves on purple cardstock with copper metallic embossing powder. Cut out, and mount with silicone glue. Add strands of angel-hair wire.

With One Stamp

KOOKABURRAS

The kookaburra chortles among the treetops in southern and eastern Australia, entertaining passers-by with its derisive laughter. Inhabitants of these areas awaken each morning to the mocking titters of this comical bird, which Australians often refer to as the "laughing jackass."

For years, this kookaburras stamp has been a bestseller. Stampers enjoy pressing the intricate image into polymer clay, cutting out its feathers from copper, or even embroidering the image with thread.

Kookaburras artwork, from top left:
Kookaburra Shaker Card by Lesley Bieniak;
Elegant Black Box by Stacey Apeitos;
Exchanging Information by Jill Smith;
Laughing Jackass by Phyllis Harrison;
Kookaburra Journal by Julie van Oosten;
In the Wild by Cathy Daulman; *Laughing*
by Ellen Eadie; *At Dusk* by Ann Grear;
Framed Kookaburras by Robyn Jaques;
and *Embroidered Kookaburras*
by Kate Mitchell.

Kookaburra sits in the ol' gum tree,
Merry merry king of the bush is he,
Laugh kookaburra, laugh,
How gay your life must be.

Kookaburra Shaker Card
Leslie Bieniak

Stamp kookaburras with black ink on white cardstock and heat set. Cut out the image, and color it with markers. On pale green cardstock, impress the flowering gum stamp randomly, using brown dye ink. On darker green cardstock, pencil in a frame, and bronze emboss the flowering gum image in top left corner. Repeat down the left side. Cut out the frame, carefully cutting around the images as shown. Mount the frame on a foam-core frame (slightly smaller to remain hidden). Adhere small gum nuts and leaves to the pale-green card, and mount the cutout kookaburras with foam tape. Inside the window area, sprinkle small gum nuts and leaves before covering the opening with acetate.

Framed Kookaburras
Robyn Jaques

Stamp kookaburras with black non-porous ink on thin sheets of craft metal, once on gold, three times on copper. Cut out the tree branch and leaves from the gold metal using sharp, pointed nail scissors. From one copper image, cut out the three foreground birds. From the second copper image, cut out the two background birds, and then cut into two pieces: the upper body with claws, and the tail with the piece of trunk attached (when assembling, the tail will tuck under the tree trunk). Using a foam mat under the metal, trace around the design lines with a fine-point stylus. Turn the piece face-down, and work the back with the larger end of the stylus to raise the features. Repeat with all pieces. Assemble with silicone caulking. From the third copper print, cut and shape one kookaburra and attach to a gum leaf. Write poem on leaf with black pen. Stamp background on green cardstock with black ink, using Australian stamp images. Color with pencils. Trace around design with a fine-point stylus. Assemble with picture frame.

Embroidered Kookaburras
Kate Mitchell

Stamp kookaburras on white cardstock. Cut into an oval shape, and color with watercolor pencils. Stamp leaves and gum nuts on separate cardstock, color, and cut out. Adhere both stamped cutouts on a green panel. Embroider gum nuts with pink floss. Adhere the finished piece to a folded rust card, adding gold corners.

Elegant Black Box
Stacey Apeitos

Stamp kookaburras with black ink into yellow polymer clay, trim the edges with a knife, and bake per package directions. When cool, accent with gold rub-ons. Trace the polymer clay shape onto the lid of a papier-mâché hatbox, then set aside. Glue string just outside the traced line, and allow to dry. Combine one part water with three parts white glue, and paint it onto the lid. Cover the wet lid with tissue paper, allowing it to wrinkle. Repeat this process with two or three sheets of tissue, and then decorate the box using the same technique. Allow both pieces to dry. With sandpaper, clean the tissue away from the rim edges of the box and lid. Paint both with black acrylics, and allow to dry. Use metallic rub-ons to accent, and seal with acrylic spray. Adhere polymer clay kookaburras to the lid, and add a bow.

At Dusk
Ann Grear

Bray rainbow colors of dye ink onto glossy cardstock, and set aside. Stamp and emboss kookaburras onto white cardstock, color with markers, and cut out. Adhere a green frame to the brayered piece, then adhere tree bark, leaves, and a yellow gum tree flower to the frame. Adhere cutout kookaburras as shown, and layer ensemble on a black card sprayed with gold spray-webbing.

With One Stamp
OPEN BOOK

Books open up worlds of inspiration, and this open book stamp provides visual proof of that. This deceptively simple Medieval-style book stamp can be used on canvas, cardstock, vellum, and a variety of papers to create everything from tote bags to gift boxes. Talented stamp artists seem to revel in the book's blank pages, using it to express their wishes, dreams, and innermost thoughts.

Open Book stamp art, from left: *Self* and *Venetian Book* by Carolyn Waitt; *Alphabet Book* by Maryse Carrier; *Journey* by Pat Pleacher; *Book Tote* by Frankie Fioretti; *Once Upon a Dream* by Barbara Close; *Manuscript* by Judi Riesch; *Potpourri Storybook Box* by Sandra Moertel; and *A Heart for Thee* by P. J. Dutton.

Manuscript
Judi Riesch

Stamp the book image on brown cardstock, once in black and again in sepia ink. Cut out. Stamp the book several times on vellum, and cut out the pages only, embossing the edges with an embossing pen and gold powder. Collage the pages with script imagery. Remove the cover from an old, discarded book, collage decorative papers onto it, and then adhere the black stamped book cover to the design. Cut the border off the sepia stamped book image, and adhere the border to the black-stamped image as shown. Assemble the stamped pages, and sew them into the spine of the book. Add a gold tassel and key charm.

Journey
Pat Pleacher

Stamp book image twice; stamp and write on one, and color in the other's details. Cut out the image with the writing and attach to the open book, using rolled paper or foam mounting tape to raise the pages. Stamp hands, color, cut out, and attach to book. Assemble the piece to black cardstock, and attach a green ribbon bookmark. Assemble on a background sheet decorated with stamps and photos, and then adhere on black cardstock.

Book Tote
Frankie Fioretti

Pre-wash and press a canvas tote bag.
Mask off the center square with masking
tape. Apply a thin wash of fabric paints
with a foam brush, dry, and press smooth.
Using darker colors, stamp fabric paint in
positions shown. Mask the upper and lower
books, and use tape to create outer borders.
Apply thinned paint. Mask borders, and
fill outer border with script background
image. Stamp large words with lower-case
alphabet. Fill book pages with stamped
face and word images, and add key
images. Press with a hot iron to heat
set the paint.

Potpourri Storybook Box
Sandra Moertel

Stamp the book image four times with black ink on colored cardstock or
on gift paper adhered to cardstock. Cut out the images. Sponge on wax shoe
polish, dry, and buff. Glue the edges together as shown to form a box, and
adhere gold cord along the top. Paint a half-pint cardboard berry basket with
gold spray paint, dry, and insert inside the book box. Fill the basket with
potpourri, and attach a burgundy bow and dried rosebud to the front.

Self
Carolyn Waitt

Stamp face using dye ink, and cut to the size of a miniature
book page. Cut three more pieces of white cardstock the
same size, inscribe a quote on one, and place that piece on
top of the other two. Color the edges. Emboss book image
in white and gold, cut out, and adhere to white mulberry
paper with torn edges. Tie charm to a bookmark ribbon,
and adhere to book as shown. Assemble piece on
buff-colored cardstock.

GLOSSARY

Acid Free: Without acid at the time of manufacture, with a pH ranging from 7.0 to 9.0. Even acid-free papers and materials can become acidic over time, leading to the weakening of cellulose in papers, causing discoloration and deterioration. The more pure the cellulose in the paper, the more permanent the paper will be.

Acid Migration: The transfer of acid from an acidic material to a less acidic or neutral-pH material. Occurs when neutral materials are exposed to human hands or atmospheric pollutants (air, water), or when two paper materials come in contact.

Acrylic: A water-soluble paint made from pigments and a plastic binder.

Alkaline: A chemical used to neutralize acids as they form within or migrate to paper. Note: High-alkaline papers are no better than high-acid papers.

Archival: Archival-quality (or conservation-quality) materials are stable or chemically balanced, suggesting durability and permanence (that is, high resistance to aging). Such materials are considered safe for preservation purposes.

Artistamp: Faux postage stamp, often created with art stamps and collage techniques. Artistamps are not meant to be used in place of regular postage; they are an art form, sometimes collectible.

Assemblage: Three-dimensional objects glued to a surface. Sometimes used in conjunction with collage and montage.

Bleed: A feathery effect that occurs when too much ink or paint is absorbed by paper.

Bone Folder: A flat piece of bone or plastic, round at one end, pointed at the other. Used for scoring and folding paper.

Brayer: A small, rubber "rolling pin" used to flatten papers, smooth surfaces, or apply paints or inks to art stamps.

Cold Pressed: A paper with slight surface texture produced by pressing the finished sheet between cold cylinders.

Collage: Papers and found objects such as ticket stubs and ephemera glued to a flat surface.

Complementary Color: Each primary color (red, blue, yellow) has a complementary, or opposite, color made by mixing the other two primaries. An example of two complementary colors: red and green.

Deckle Edge: The natural feathery edge of paper; the result of the runoff of wet pulp when making handmade paper. Handmade paper has four deckle edges; machine-made papers usually have two.

Gel Medium: See polymer medium (below).

Gesso: An opaque, chalk-like base used to prepare surfaces for painting, lettering, gilding, etc.

Gouache: Opaque watercolor (a colored pigment with a gum binder and opaque filler).

Gum Arabic: A plant resin used to bind color pigments. Improves paint flow and adds gloss.

Handmade Paper: Paper made by hand using a mold, which is a frame covered with a flat, rigid (Western) or flexible (Oriental) screen. The mold is covered by a flat frame called a deckle to contain the runoff of wet pulp, then dipped into a vat of wet pulp, shaken to distribute the fibers evenly, and drained of excess water. The remaining wet mat of fibers forms the sheet of paper, which is pressed and dried using various methods.

Hot Glue Sticks: Solid sticks of glue in clear, white, and colors (some with glitter), used with a hot glue gun.

Hot Pressed: A smooth, glazed paper surface produced by pressing a finished sheet of paper through hot cylinders.

Inks: Colored pigment suspended in various soluble and insoluble binders. Inks tend not to be lightfast as other media.

Interference Pigment: Metal oxides or particles of mica which cause an iridescence or luster when mixed with acrylic paints.

Kozo: Long, tough fiber from the mulberry tree that produces strong, absorbent paper known as Kozo or mulberry paper. Kozo is the most common fiber used in Japanese papermaking.

Layout: The arrangement of heading, text, illustration, and artwork on a page.

Lightfastness: The degree and speed with which a pigment or colored paper fades in sunlight.

Machine-Made Paper: Paper made on a rapid-running machine called a Fourdrinier, producing consistently uniform quantities of sheets or rolls.

Marbled Paper: A technique of applying patterns, resembling marble textures, to paper.

Methyl Cellulose (Wallpaper Paste): A pure adhesive that dries clear. Suitable for archival mounting.

Mixed Media: The use of several media (such as paints, papers, rubber stamps, inks) to create a work of art.

Mold-Made (or Mould-Made) Paper: Paper made by slowly rotating a cylinder mold that simulates the process of making paper by hand.

Montage: A work of art incorporating photographs into a collage.

Mulberry Paper: See Kozo (above).

Mylar: A protective, clear polyester covering for photos and album pages; the highest quality material used for this purpose.

Opaque: A surface lacking clarity (cannot be seen through) that does not transmit light rays.

Papyrus: A paper-like material made from the pithy inner stem of a large, aquatic plant from the sedge family.

Parchment: Animal skins or linings stretched and prepared as a writing or painting surface.

Paste-up: Assemblage of cut-up elements of a piece of work, stuck onto paper to finalize a layout.

Permanence: The degree to which a paper's properties resist deterioration or change over time. An assessment of permanence also must consider storage and end-use conditions: Even a paper with a 4.0 acid pH will last indefinitely if stored under ideal conditions.

pH: A measure of the concentration of acidity or alkalinity in paper. The scale runs from 1 pH (very high acid content), through 7 pH (balanced, neutral), to 14 pH (very high alkaline content). Buffered papers range from 7 to 9 pH.

Polymer Medium: A protective acrylic liquid used as an adhesive for light- to middleweight papers; also used as a varnish for decoupage. Glossy and dull matte finishes are available.

PVA (Polyvinyl Acetate): An archival white glue that is stronger than gel medium. It mixes well with gloss medium. Transparent even after many coats, it always will remain water soluble. Mixed with gel, it becomes water resistant.

Rag Paper: Paper made from cotton or linen rag (textile) fiber. Once made into thread, these fibers are longer, tougher, and somewhat hardened. Rag papers contain from 50- to 100-percent cotton fiber pulp, which is indicated as a percentage of the total fiber content.

Ream: 500 sheets of paper.

Recycled Paper: Paper made from post-consumer waste.

Rice Paper: A misnomer used to describe lightweight Oriental papers. There is no such thing as "rice paper," but rice straw occasionally is mixed with other fibers in Asian papermaking, and rice starch is used to size papers made from kozo (mulberry), gampi, and mitsumata fibers.

Shade: A color made by adding black to any hue.

Tempera: Colored pigment with several binders that render the paint opaque. Like gouache, tempera is water soluble even after drying.

Tint: A color made by adding white to any opaque color.

Tone: The shade gradations from white to black, or from light to dark.

Translucent: Describes a quality between transparent and opaque; objects can be seen through translucent objects but without clarity.

Vellum: A finely textured paper surface; a term also used to designate heavyweight, translucent drawing, or crafting papers.

Watercolor: Colored pigment mixed with gum arabic binder. Usually transparent and water-soluble after dry.

Watercolor Paper: A 100-percent cotton rag-quality paper. Comes in light, medium, and heavy weights, as well as surface textures such as hot pressed (smooth) and cold pressed (rough).

Wheat Paste: Also known as wallpaper paste; the preferred archival adhesive of bookbinders.

RESOURCES
Art Stamp Companies

Acey Deucy
P.O. Box 194
Ancram, NY 12502
U.S.
Phone: (518) 398-5108
Fax: (518) 398-6364

ERA Graphics
2476 Ottawa Way
San Jose, CA 95130
U.S.
Phone: (408) 364-1124
Fax: (408) 364-1126

Fred Mullett
Rubber Stamps From Nature Prints
2707 59th Southwest, Suite A
Seattle, WA 98116
U.S.
Phone: (206) 932-9482
Fax: (206) 932-8462

Hero Arts
1343 Powell Street
Emeryville, CA 94608
U.S.
Phone: (800) 822-4376
Fax: (800) 441-3632
www.heroarts.com

Hot Potatoes
2805 Columbine Place
Nashville, TN 37204
U.S.
Phone: (615) 269-8002
Fax: (615) 269-8004
www.hotpotatoes.com

Impress Me Rubber Stamps
17116 Escalon Drive
Encino, CA 91436-4030
U.S.
Phone: (818) 907-1486
e-mail: Impressme@earthlink.net

Judi-Kins
17803 South Hobart Boulevard
Gardena, CA 90248
U.S.
Phone: (310) 515-1115

Krafty Lady
Rear 9 Edgewood Road
Dandenong, Victoria 3175
Australia
Phone/Fax: (613) 9794-6064
www.kraftylady.com.au

Limited Edition
1514 Stafford Street
Redwood City, CA 94063
U.S.
Phone: (650) 299-9700
Fax: (650) 261-9300

Magenta Rubber Stamps
351 Blain
Mont Saint-Hilaire, Quebec J3H 3B4
Canada
Phone: (800) 565-5254
Fax: (514) 464-6353

Ornamentum
32903 30th Avenue Southwest
Federal Way, WA 98023
U.S.
Phone: (206) 838-3259

Paper Parachute
P.O. Box 91385
Portland, OR 97291-0385
U.S.
Phone: (503) 531-0489
e-mail: Raymond.Werner@intel.com

Personal Stamp Exchange
360 Sutton Place
Santa Rosa, CA 95407
U.S.
Phone: (707) 588-8058
Fax: (707) 588-7476

Red Head Stamp
P.O. Box 3374
Bellevue, WA 98009
U.S.
Phone: (206) 660-2028
Fax: (888) 727-8267
e-mail: Redhead206@aol.com

Rubber Poet
Box 218
Rockville, UT 84763
U.S.
Phone: (435) 772-3441
Fax: (800) 906-7638
www.wyoming.com/~cavenewt/pigs/

Rubber Stampede
P.O. Box 246
Berkeley, CA 94701
U.S.
Phone: (800) 632-8386
www.rubberstampede.com

Stamp Francisco –
Coco Stamp
1248 9th Avenue
San Francisco, CA 94122
U.S.
Phone: (415) 566-1018
www.stampfrancisco.com

Stamp Out Cute
7084 North Cedar, #137
Fresno, CA 93720
U.S.

Stamp Zia
29205 Elm Island
Waterford, WI 53185
U.S.
Phone: (414) 534-6039
www.stampzia.com

Stampendous!
1357 South Lewis Street
Anaheim, CA 92805
U.S.
Phone: (714) 563-9501
Fax: (714) 563-9509
www.stampendous.com

Stampin' Up!
U.S.
Phone: (800) 782-6787
www.stampinup.com

Stampington & Company,
LLC
22992 Mill Creek, Suite B
Laguna Hills, CA 92653
U.S.
Phone: (949) 380-7318
Fax: (949) 380-9355
www.stampington.com

Stamp-It Rubber Stamps
P.O. Box 653
Victoria Park, Western Australia 6979
Australia
Phone: (618) 9470-5422
Fax: (618) 9361-0547
www.stampit.com.au

Stamps Happen, Inc.
419 South Acacia Avenue
Fullerton, CA 92831
U.S.
Phone: (714) 879-9894
Fax: (714) 879-9896

ThINKING Stamps
4/186 Main Road
Blackwood, South Australia 5051
Australia
Phone: (618) 8370-3722

Tin Can Mail -
Primary Resource
U.S.
Phone: (650) 367-1177

Toybox Rubber Stamps
P.O. Box 1487
Healdsburg, CA 95448
U.S.
Phone: (707) 431-1400
Fax: (707) 431-2408

Zettiology
P.O. Box 2665
Renton, WA 98056
U.S.
Phone: (206) 255-1543

Supplies

Aiko's Art Materials (paper)
3347 North Clark
Chicago, IL 60657
U.S.
Phone: (773) 404-5600

A Lost Art
(sealing wax and seals)
P.O. Box 1338
Baldwin Park, CA 91706
U.S.
Phone: (818) 790-2125

Cartoon Colour Company,
Inc. (cel-vinyl paint)
9024 Lindblade Street
Culver City, CA 90232
U.S.
Phone: (213) 838-8467

Clearsnap, Inc.
(ColorBox inks)
Box 98
Anacortes, WA 98221
U.S.
Phone: (360) 293-6634
Fax: (360) 293-6699
www.clearsnap.com

Daniel Smith, Inc.
(art materials)
P.O. Box 84268
Seattle, WA 98124-5568
U.S.
Phone: (206) 223-9599
Fax: (206) 224-0404

Fascinating Folds (papers)
P.O. Box 10070
Glendale, AZ 85318
U.S.
Phone: (602) 375-9978
Fax: (602) 375-9979
www.fascinating-folds.com

Fiskars, Inc.
(scissors, punches)
7811 West Stewart Avenue
Wausau, WI 54401
U.S.
Phone: (715) 842-2091
www.fiskars.com

Greg Markim, Inc.
(papermaking kits)
P.O. Box 13245
Milwaukee, WI 53213
U.S.
Phone: (414) 453-1480

Green Heron Book Arts
(bookmaking kits)
1928 21st Avenue, Suite A
Forest Grove, OR 97116
U.S.
Phone: (503) 357-7263
www.green-heron-kits.com

The Japanese Paper Place
(papers)
887 Queen Street West
Toronto, Ontario M6J 1G5
Canada
Phone: (416) 703-0089
Fax: (416) 703-0163

Loose Ends (papers)
P.O. Box 20310
Salem, OR 97307
U.S.
Phone: (503) 390-7457
Fax: (503) 390-4724
www.4loosends.com

Marvy-Uchida (markers)
1027 East Burgrove Street
Carson, CA 90746
U.S.
Phone: (800) 541-5877

Papers by Catherine
(papers)
11328 South Post Oak Road, #108
Houston, TX 77035
U.S.
Phone: (713) 723-3334
Fax: (713) 723-4749

Quire Handmade Paper
(papers)
P.O. Box 248
Belair, South Australia 5052
Australia
Phone/Fax: (618) 8295-2966

Ranger Industries (ink)
15 Park Road
Tinton Falls, NJ 07724
U.S.
Phone: (732) 389-3535
Fax: (732) 389-1102

Speedball
(opaque markers)
Hunt Manufacturing Co.
Statesville, NC 28677
U.S.
Phone: (704) 872-9511

Suze Weinberg
(mixed media)
39 Old Bridge Drive
Howell, NJ 07731
U.S.
Phone: (732) 364-3136
Fax: (732) 364-7244
www.schmoozewithsuze.com

Tsukineko (ink)
15411 Northeast 95th Street
Redmond, WA 98052
U.S.
Phone: (800) 769-6633
Fax: (425) 883-7418
www.tsukineko.com

USArtQuest, Inc.
(mixed media)
17980 Spruce Run
Chelsea, MI 48118
U.S.
Phone: (800) 200-7848
Fax: (734) 475-7224
www.USArtQuest.com

Magazines

The Rubber Gazette
6 Ailsa Court
Alexander Heights, Western Australia
6064
Australia
Phone: (618) 9342-0054
Fax: (618) 9247-3665

Rubberstampmadness
408 Southwest Monroe, #210
Corvallis, OR 97330
U.S.
Phone: (541) 752-0075
Fax: (541) 752-5475
www.rubberstampmadness.com

Somerset Studio
22992 Mill Creek, Suite B
Laguna Hills, CA 92653
U.S.
Phone: (949) 380-7318
Fax: (949) 380-9355
www.somersetstudio.com

The Stampers' Sampler
22992 Mill Creek, Suite B
Laguna Hills, CA 92653
U.S.
Phone: (949) 380-7318
Fax: (949) 380-9355
www.stampington.com

Stamping & Papercrafting
Express Publications Pty Ltd.
2 Stanley Street
Silverwater, New South Wales 2128
Australia
Phone: (612) 9748-0599

DIRECTORY OF ARTISTS

The following individuals, who are among the finest stamp artists working today, contributed their talents to making this book. Many make art samples for product manufacturers and teach workshops on stamp-art techniques.

Stacey Apeitos
South Oakley, Victoria
Australia
Sapeitos@netlink.net.au

Anne Bagby
Winchester, TN
U.S.
Abagby@edge.net

Sherry Barncastle
Henderson, NV
U.S.

Lesley Bieniak
Keysborough, Victoria
Australia

Maryse Carrier
Mont Saint-Hilaire
Canada

Zana Clark
Waterford, WI
U.S.
Zclark@meandaur.com

Barbara Close
La Mirada, CA
U.S.

Cathy Daulman
North Perth, Western Australia
Australia

Michele DeMayo
San Diego, CA
U.S.

Robin Dudley-Howes
Redondo Beach, CA
U.S.

P. J. Dutton
Festus, MO
U.S.
Pjstamps@aol.com

Ellen Eadie
Camberwell, Victoria
Australia
eadie@eisa.net.au

Anna Leisa Ely
Tavares, FL
U.S.
AnnaElyCM@aol.com

Lea Everse
Lubbock, TX
U.S.
Lazystampr@aol.com

Jill Post Fasken
Palisade, CO
U.S.

Frankie Fioretti
Wading River, NY
U.S.

Ann Grear
Coromandel East, South Australia
Australia

Phyllis Harrison
Bomaderry, New South Wales
Australia

Janet Hofacker
Meridian, ID
U.S.
dhofacker@netscape.net

Robyn Jaques
Ashgrove, Queensland
Australia

Sherrill Kahn
Encino, CA
U.S.
Impressme@earthlink.net

Diane Lewis
Plano, TX
U.S.
Moongdz888@aol.com

MaryJo McGraw
Gardena, CA
U.S.

Hélène Métivier
Mont Saint-Hilaire, Quebec
Canada

Nathalie Métivier
Mont Saint-Hilaire, Quebec
Canada

Kate Mitchell
Ferntree Gully, Victoria
Australia

Sandra Moertel
Conneautville, PA
U.S.

Lynne Grant Mohr
Potomac, MD
U.S.
lynnem@erols.com

Tracy Moore
Renton, WA
U.S.

Julie van Oosten
Alexander Heights, Western Australia
Australia
eureka@icenet.com.au

Lynne Perrella
Ancram, NY
U.S.

Pat Pleacher
Rineyville, KY
U.S.

Lisa Renner
McKinney, TX
U.S.
Lrenner@ix.netcom.com

Judi Riesch
Atlanta, GA
U.S.

Shelley Rymer
Santa Ynez, CA
U.S.

Moya Scaddan
Sorrento, Western Australia
Australia

Jill Smith
Nunawading, Victoria
Australia

Martha Thurlow
Vineyard Haven, MA
U.S.

Sylvia Valle
Lake Forest, CA
U.S.

Carolyn Waitt
Huntington Beach, CA
U.S.

Linda Yang-Wright
Newport Beach, CA
U.S.

STAMP CREDITS

Nature Stamping
Alphabet stamps: Hero Arts

Faux Finishes
Fred Mullett, Rubber Stamps From Nature Prints

Marbled Surfaces
Background stamp: Judi-Kins

Bird stamp: Paper Parachute

Patterned Backgrounds
Magenta Rubber Stamps

**Masking, Layering,
and Stenciling**
Magenta Rubber Stamps

Reverse Stamping
Lotus stamp: Judi-Kins

Egyptian woman: Red Head Stamp

Faux Postage
Stamp Out Cute

Deep Thermal Embossing
Acey Deucy

Stamping on Acetate
Magenta Rubber Stamps

Metallic Accents
Marble texture cube stamp: Stampendous!

Spiral stamp and collage figure: Acey Deucy

Papyrus background stamp: Judi-Kins

Collage and Decoupage
Acey Deucy

Stamped Booklets
Impress Me Rubber Stamps

Miniature Books
Acey Deucy

Large-Format Art
Stamp Zia

With One Stamp: Cranes
Judi-Kins

With One Stamp: Grapevines
Stampin' Up!

With One Stamp: Kookaburras
Krafty Lady

With One Stamp: Open Book
Stampington & Company, LLC

ACKNOWLEDGMENTS

A book such as this is truly a collaborative effort, and many talented individuals deserve acknowledgment. First, I want to say "thank you" to everyone who had a hand in this endeavor—from artists, to editors, to photographers and printers. You know who you are, and I hope you know how vital your contribution was to this book and how greatly I appreciate it.

Having said this, it's time to list a few names. But let me preface that by saying these are not just names; these are the creative, dedicated people responsible for producing the book you now hold in your hands. I consider myself very fortunate to have known and worked with them. First, the artists.

All 41 stamp artists whose work is represented in this book are to be commended for their talent and industry. In particular, I extend my deepest appreciation to the 13 artists who contributed their projects to each chapter and additional artwork to the galleries. A double "thank you" to Lea Everse, who contributed two projects. Anyone who knows Lea will hardly be surprised!

To Janet Hofacker, thank you for sharing your beautiful, inspiring nature journals. To Lynne Grant Mohr, I extend my gratitude for turning in such a gorgeous project well ahead of schedule; it persuaded the publishers to expand this book.

To sisters Nathalie and Hélène Métivier, thank you for contributing your unique slant on stamping and preparing background papers. Your work is incomparable!

To Moya Scaddan and Linda Yang-Wright, I appreciate your flexibility and willingness to quickly turn in such high-caliber projects so near my deadline. *Stamp Art* would be incomplete without you.

To Diane Lewis, I appreciate the ways you lent your support, encouragement, and talent to this project. I'm delighted to count you among my friends.

To Sherrill Kahn, Lynne Perrella, and Lisa Renner—superior stamp artists all—thank you for teaching us to use stamps artistically, combine them with mixed media and collage, and make life more beautiful. Zana Clark, you've taught us to enlarge our view of stamping, taking it "beyond cards" into the realm of gallery artwork.

And to my friend, Julie van Oosten, thank you for sharing your passion for art stamps, miniatures, and book arts. You inspire me with your talent and generosity.

Now, the wordsmiths:

To Carol Meredith, thank you for coordinating this project so deftly and with such a great attitude. You kept me on my toes! To Martha Wetherill and Shawna Mullen, I'm grateful for the way you planned and oversaw this book so well, and for your patience, faith, and good humor throughout.

To my agent, Marilyn Howard of Creative Freelancers, thank you for giving me this opportunity.

Lastly, I gratefully acknowledge the publisher of *Somerset Studio* magazine, Kellene Giloff. Thank you, Kellene, for introducing me to the wonderful world of stamp art. Thank you for allowing me to edit your beautiful magazine these past two years; it is a privilege, one I never take for granted.

ABOUT THE AUTHOR

Sharilyn Miller is the editor of *Somerset Studio*, a bimonthly magazine for art stampers, book artists, papercrafters, and lettering artists. Geared to intermediate and advanced artists, this highly visual magazine covers the latest in stamping techniques and creativity.

Sharilyn became editor of *Somerset Studio* shortly before it was launched in January 1997. Previously, she worked for several years as a reporter with *The Orange County Register* in Santa Ana, California. Sharilyn holds a commercial art degree from the Northwest College of Art, Poulsbo, Washington, and a communications degree from California State University, Fullerton.